THE
MINIRTH
GUIDE
FOR
CHRISTIAN
COUNSELORS

THE
MINIRTH
GUIDE
FOR
CHRISTIAN
COUNSELORS

Frank MINIRTH

BROADMAN
&HOLMAN
PUBLISHERS

Nashville, Tennessee

0–8054–2799–6

Published by Broadman & Holman Publishers
Nashville, Tennessee

Scripture quotations are identified by the following acronyms:
KJV, King James Version. NASB, the New American Standard Bible, © the Lockman
Foundation, 1960, 1962, 1963, 1968, 1971, 1972, 1973, 1975, 1977; used by permission.
NIV, The Holy Bible, New International Version, copyright © 1973, 1978, 1984 by
International Bible Society. NKJV, New King James Version, copyright © 1979, 1980, 1982,
Thomas Nelson, Inc., Publishers. NRSV, New Revised Standard Version of the Bible, copy-
right © 1989 by the Division of Christian Education of the National Council of Churches
of Christ in the United States of America, used by permission, all rights reserved. RSV,
Revised Standard Version of the Bible, copyrighted 1946, 1952, © 1971, 1973.

Dewey Decimal Classification: 253.5
Subject Heading: COUNSELING—RELIGIOUS ASPECTS

2 3 4 5 6 7 8 9 10 08 07 06 05 04 03

Dedicated to Dr. Cecil Johnson,
a truly godly person,
who encouraged me to
write this book

Contents

Preface

What is Christian counseling? It could be defined as "the ministry of one individual seeking to help another person in accordance with the Word of God." It is built on certain premises without which there is no true Christian counseling. These premises include: man without Christ is lost, and sin still needs to be emphasized.

An important concept in Christian counseling is the makeup of man: spirit, soul, and body. Neither view of dichotomies or trichotomies negate the need for Christian counseling.

Since Christian counseling hinges on the term *counsel,* this concept is analyzed biblically with both Greek and Hebrew words.

Fundamental to Christian counseling is growth in Christ. Many problems in counseling abate with growth in Christ. Thus, basic principles that seem so simple, such as Bible study, prayer, fellowship, and witnessing, become of paramount importance.

Certain emotions such as anxiety, guilt, anger, and depression seem to arise more often than other emotions in Christian counseling. These common emotions are carefully analyzed, and biblical solutions are offered.

The Christian counselor needs specifics on exactly how to do Christian counseling. After offering seven biblical steps for doing Christian counseling, the pieces are pulled together with a discussion of why Christians break down and how the Christian counselor can help. Also, several examples of biblical homework assignments are offered.

Finally, the Christian counselor is often in need of quick reference material. Much is included. This reference material can range from important phone numbers to DSM-IV coding system of mental disorders; an overview of various secular psychotherapies from a Christian perspective is also given.

In short, it seems the Christian world is lacking and in need of a book that would include material from the theoretical to the practical with actual forms to establish a Christian counseling or mentoring ministry. I trust this book does just that. Whether a counselor needs just a few forms or a complete system, this book includes it.

1

Basic Principles
of Christian Counseling

What is Christian counseling? *Christian counseling* could be defined as "the ministry of one individual seeking to help another person recognize, understand, and solve his or her own problems in accordance with the Word of God." The emphasis in the above definition is on only two individuals—the patient and the therapist. This emphasis is valid, yet Christian counseling has even further implications. The entire body of Christ in a local area has a responsibility to minister to the emotional needs of one of its members, and the counselor will do well to take advantage in therapy of the great rehabilitative resources available in the local church.

The Uniqueness of Christian Counseling

Whether one thinks of the entire local church or the one-to-one relationship when Christian counseling is mentioned, and whether the Christian counselor is a minister, psychologist, psychiatrist, or social worker, certain principles make Christian counseling unique.

First, it accepts the Bible as the final standard of authority. As a result, Christians are not left to explore and dissect through the myriad of philosophies and their own logic and to hope by chance to hit upon a correct system of right and wrong.

Furthermore, Christians do not have to depend totally upon their own consciences to direct their behavior. They may rely on the Word of God. If one's conscience agrees with the Word of God, then the conscience is valid; if not, the conscience is invalid. For example, in some cultures a man might feel guilty for seeing his wife in the nude. Should such a man be told to live up to his conscience? His conscience is too strict and should be reeducated according to the Word of God. As mentioned above, in other cases an individual may have too little conscience because of poor identity figures. Thus, he may have developed the attitude that society and others are bad and whatever he does to them is all right. In contrast to the former example, this is a case of a too-weak conscience, which also needs reeducating according to the Word of God.

Thus, Christian counseling offers not only practical guidelines through the Bible, but also it points to one final standard of authority—the Bible. All schools of thought in psychiatry need a foundation and framework from which to build. The Bible is that foundation for Christian counselors.

The Bible is not primarily a book of rules on rights and wrongs. It is meant to give guidelines, spiritual nourishment, and life. The Lord Jesus Christ expressed this concept well when he stated, "The words that I speak unto you, they are spirit, and they are life" (John 6:63 KJV).

The Bible gives Christian counselors a foundation and a framework. It not only gives insights into human behavior; it puts everything into proper perspective. It tells who man is, where man came from, the purpose of man, and the nature of man. By joining this foundation with the scientific facts and observations of psychiatry, the Christian counselor has a good vantage point from which to help people solve problems.

The Power of the Holy Spirit

Christian counseling is unique because it depends not only on man's willpower to be responsible but also on God's enabling, indwelling power of the Holy Spirit to conquer man's problems. We do not wish to imply that man has no responsibility for his actions, for he does; yet many Christians choose to act irresponsibly. However, our willingness and attempts to be responsible must be joined with God's power. Through God's power, man need no longer be a slave to a weak will, his past environment, or social situations. Problems do not disappear when a person accepts Christ, but there is a new power to deal with them.

The Godly Components

Christian counseling is unique because, even though man does have a basic selfish component, he, if a Christian, has a much stronger godly component. In Romans 7:23, Paul gave the description of an internal battle in an individual. The description is that of a good law in the individual mind waging war against an evil law in its members. As a result, the will is overpowered by the evil law, and only through the Spirit of Christ is victory obtained. Also, only through the Spirit of Christ can real spiritual insights be obtained. The apostle Paul stated, "But the natural man receiveth not the things of the Spirit of God: for they are foolishness unto him: neither can he know them, because they are spiritually discerned" (1 Cor. 2:14 KJV). In Greek the *natural* man means the *psychological* man.

The Time Factor

Christian counseling is unique in that it offers an effective way to deal with the past as well as the present. Some of the older schools of thought deal almost exclusively with the past, while some of the newer schools of thought in psychiatry deal mostly with the present. Christian counselors can deal with both. The following two verses point to only a couple of ways that can be very effective in dealing with past guilt or worries: "If we confess our sins, He is faithful and right-eous to forgive us our sins and to cleanse us from all unrighteousness" (1 John 1:9 NASB). "One thing I do: forgetting what lies behind and reaching forward to what lies ahead, I press on" (Phil. 3:13–14 NASB). Of course, the counselor cannot always expect a client to get well by sim-ply pointing out these verses; he must work with each person individually as he helps the per-son gain insight and victory over his problems.

God's Love

Christian counseling is unique because it is based on God's love. The apostle John stated, "In this is love, not that we loved God, but that He loved us and sent His Son to be the propiti-ation for our sins" (1 John 4:10 NASB). Because God loved us, and His love flows through us, we love others and feel a responsibility toward them. Again the apostle John states, "Whoever loves the Father loves the child born of Him" (1 John 5:1 NASB). The Christian counselor feels a spir-itual relationship with other Christians and hopes to help them grow in Christ as they solve their problems. The Christian counselor hopes the non-Christian accepts the Lord. Christ died for this individual, and his first step to finding real inner peace is through knowing Christ.

Universal Application

Christian counseling is unique because it is universal. It can apply to all people regardless of genetic, social, educational, or cultural background. The psychoanalytic school, the transac-tional analysts, the reality therapists—all recognize that there are certain types of people they can help better than others. Christ claimed he could help all who would turn to him (see Matt. 11:28; John 6:37). Of course, this does not mean that Christian counselors can help all people but that Christ forms the foundation of their counseling, and he can help all who are willing to turn to him.

The Whole-Person Concept

Christian counseling is unique because it seeks to deal with the whole person. The Christian counselor knows that the physical, psychological, and spiritual aspects of man are all intricately related and that when one aspect is affected, the other two are also. For example, an ulcer may start on a physical level. Some individuals have a defect in their stomach lining and have a type of bacteria known as H. Pylori; they are predisposed to ulcers. Also, a person may be prone to being a serious personality, plagued by fears and worry, which worsens the ulcer. Finally, some spiritual crisis occurs that relates to an area of chosen sin or possibly an issue of deep doubt that drives a wedge between the individual and his relationship with his Creator. Physical, psychological, and spiritual factors have now all combined to form the problem facing the counselor.

Five Biblical Principles Essential to Christian Counseling

Finally, Christian counseling is unique because of certain imperative, paramount, basic bib-lical principles. Without these basics a Christian counselor is no longer unique, no longer gifted, no longer any better than a secular counselor with an equal IQ. These principles are as follows:

1. **Man without Christ is lost.** If the counselor is to be of any practical help to his clients, he must begin with a thorough knowledge of the nature of man. Fundamental to understanding the nature of man is the realization that man without Christ is lost. To ignore a counselee's eternal destiny while helping him to solve his present problems is utterly illogical. Man without Christ is lost (John 14:6) and eternally doomed to a literal hell (Matt. 10:28; 2 Thess. 1:9). Knowledge of that fact must underlie the whole counseling process. Compelled by the love of Christ (2 Cor. 5:14), the Christian counselor desires to see the counselee come to salvation by simply trusting that Christ died for his sins (John 1:12; Rom. 6:23). Surely nothing has ever offered greater potential for solving problems and resolved more conflicts than freely accepting what Christ has done (John 6:37; Eph. 2:8–9). The Christian counselor earnestly hopes that each of his clients will one day be as open to receiving Christ as was Charlotte Elliott when she wrote the hymn "Just As I Am."

> Just as I am, without one plea,
> But that Thy blood was shed for me,
> And that Thou bidd'st me come to Thee,
> O Lamb of God, I come! I come!
>
> Just as I am, and waiting not
> To rid my soul of one dark blot,
> To Thee whose blood can cleanse each spot,
> O Lamb of God, I come! I come!
>
> Just as I am, though tossed about
> With many a conflict, many a doubt,
> Fightings within and fears without,
> O Lamb of God, I come! I come!
>
> Just as I am, Thou wilt receive,
> Wilt welcome, pardon, cleanse, relieve,
> Because Thy promise I believe,
> O Lamb of God, I come! I come!

2. **Man without Christ is incomplete.** Not only is man lost without Christ; he is also incomplete. When left to himself, man faces many conflicts and an existential loneliness. He lacks the deepest comfort and most powerful resource in the universe for solving problems—Jesus Christ. When a person trusts Christ as his Savior, the Holy Spirit comes to indwell (2 Cor. 3:16–17), empower (Eph. 3:16), guide (Rom. 8:14), teach (John 14:26), and free from sin and death (Rom. 8:2). Upon receiving Christ as Savior, man literally has the resources of God himself available for living life (John 15:4–7) and coping with his problems (1 Pet. 5:7). The negative impact

of conflicts will be greatly reduced as one learns to walk closely with God. Among biblical examples of people who benefited immeasurably from a close walk with God are Moses (Exod. 33), Hezekiah (2 Kings 18), Asaph (Ps. 73), and the apostle Paul (Phil. 3). Our overwhelming need for Christ to bring a sense of completion to our lives has been well expressed in an old hymn by Annie S. Hawks and Robert Lowry.

> I need Thee every hour,
> Most gracious Lord;
> No tender voice like Thine
> Can peace afford.
>
> I need Thee every hour,
> Stay Thou near by;
> Temptations lose their power
> When Thou art nigh.
>
> I need Thee every hour,
> In joy or pain;
> Come quickly and abide,
> Or life is vain.
>
> I need Thee every hour,
> Most Holy One;
> O make me Thine indeed,
> Thou blessed Son.
>
> I need Thee, O I need Thee;
> Every hour I need Thee!
> O bless me now, my Savior;
> I come to Thee!

Psychiatric research indicates that if a child is to be healthy he must feel that his parents will meet his dependency needs and never reject him. Certainly the same holds true for a child in the family of God. Understanding that man has certain dependency needs which only God can be expected to meet will have a large bearing on the counseling process.

Jane was a young woman thirty years of age who was experiencing depression as a result of marital conflicts. She did not know Christ and had no human resources to whom she could turn. She had become desperate and was considering suicide. During a course of therapy, she came to trust Christ. She began to receive support from the body of Christ. Many situational problems continued. However, she could now withstand the stress from without because Christ was within. In her own words, "I accepted Jesus Christ as my Lord and Savior after being hospitalized twice for depression and anxiety. In the past I had refused to look inward and acknowledge my self-centeredness. I made impossible demands on my loved ones in order that I might achieve happiness. But a person can love with a Christlike nature only from a secure position of accepting himself and others for what they are, as they are."

3. **Man is depraved.** Closely tied in with man's lostness and incompleteness without Christ is the fact that man is depraved. He is not basically good. Although he may have some consciousness of right and wrong (Rom. 2:14–15), may not be as sinful as he could be (2 Tim. 3:13), and may perform some good works (Isa. 64:6), he is still depraved. No human being is without sin (Rom. 3:9–20); man has an innate tendency to evil (Rom. 7:14–25) and, of course, can never satisfy God though he may attempt to establish his own righteousness (Rom. 10:3). Even after he accepts Christ, he is still depraved. Although he now has a new nature, he is still being pulled toward sin by the dangerous old nature (Rom. 7:20; Gal. 5:17; Eph. 4:22–24).

The counselor who recognizes that man is by nature depraved knows that attempts at "self-actualization" will ultimately fail. That is, man in himself has neither the capability nor the goodness necessary to solve his own problems and overcome the evil within him. The Christian counselor agrees with Jeremiah's assessment that "the heart is more deceitful than all else and is desperately sick; who can understand it?" (Jer. 17:9 NASB). The mind is dishonest and tricky. Man employs various defense mechanisms in efforts to avoid taking an honest look at himself.

Rationalization is one of the more common defense mechanisms. For example, an individual may declare, "I simply don't love my mate anymore. Surely God doesn't want me to stay in a marriage with someone I don't love." Actually, the individual may be having an affair and trying to find a plausible excuse for his behavior. He is entangled in sin. The Christian counselor will always be aware that depravity is an integral part of the nature of man.

4. **Man is under attack.** Not only is man lost, incomplete, and depraved, but he is under constant attack by a most powerful enemy—Satan. Satan is more powerful, clever, and shrewd than most people realize. C. S. Lewis captured some of the craftiness of Satan most effectively in his best-selling *Screwtape Letters*.

Satan desires that nonbelievers stay in spiritual darkness (John 3:19–21). He also prowls about seeking to destroy the mental health of Christians (Eph. 6:11–16; 1 Pet. 5:8–9). There are various devices Satan uses to accomplish these purposes. He can deceive, enticing people to pay attention to false doctrines (1 Tim. 4:1–3). He can influence thinking, causing man to focus on his own interests rather than on God's (Matt. 16:21–23). Satan can hinder the spread of the gospel (1 Thess. 2:2, 14–16). He can tempt (1 Cor. 7:5). He can oppress people mentally, even to the point of driving them insane (Luke 8:26–39).

Although demonic possession is possible, Satan usually chooses to work in far more subtle ways. For example, he best accomplishes his purposes with Christians by tempting them over and over in the area of their greatest weakness, whether materialism, pride, lust, a tendency toward depression, or whatever. The great variety of Satan's schemes is another factor of which the Christian counselor should be constantly aware.

5. **Man is sinful.** Finally, not only is man lost, incomplete, depraved, and under attack, but he is also sinful. When was the last time you heard a sermon on sin? When was the last time you

heard a sermon on hell? When was the last time you heard a sermon like Jonathan Edwards's "Sinners in the Hands of an Angry God"? Has it been a while? I suspect it has. As a child, I recall hearing sermon after sermon on sin, but not so today. Without this concept there is no right or wrong, there is no moral compass, there is no Christian counseling. Without a foundation in the dangers and elusiveness of sin, the Christian counselor will be ineffective for Christ. Whatever happened to sin? I have studied the topic from several dimensions. I believe that at least eleven reasons account for the demise of the concept of sin.

1   People will want less and less to hear about sin as time progresses. The topics people want to hear are certainly not about sin. "For the time will come when they will not endure sound doctrine; but wanting to have their ears tickled, they will accumulate for themselves teachers in accordance to their own desires" (2 Tim. 4:3 NASB). Whatever happened to sin? Is it that people do not want to hear it?

2   People have become more and more focused on individual money issues that affect them and less and less on moral and sin issues. I hate the popular slogan of today that has been said to characterize our society, "It's the economy, stupid." Polls reveal that a majority of people in our society say that it does not matter what a person does in his or her private life as long as the economy is doing well. Money takes precedence over morals. Whatever happened to sin? Did money buy it out?

3   People have bought psychology hook, line, and sinker. Around the turn of the century, Sigmund Freud emphasized some principles that may have been carried too far at times. Man's sinful behavior shifted from what he had done to why he had done it—issues with parents? Issues of subconscious drives? Issues of repressed memories? Issues of transference? The emphasis was carried too far. As a culture we moved away from individual responsibility, choice, and sin. Whatever happened to sin? Did psychology excuse it?

4   Is the age of the evangelists (Edwards, Finney, Moody, Sunday, and Graham) fading as a movement? What great young evangelist do you know today who is on the horizon and is preaching against sin like the evangelists of old? Times have been changing, and sin has been fading. Whatever happened to sin? Have the great adversaries of sin faded?

5   Television, movies, books, magazines, and the Internet have desensitized people to sin. Sins that were once shameful have become acceptable and promoted behaviors. If sins are seen enough, they become more acceptable, and individuals become desensitized to them. Whatever happened to sin? Is sin no longer considered sin?

6   New medical advances explained new dimensions that were hard to refute. What does one do with the almost irrefutable research on the genetic aspects of many irresponsible behaviors? I believe we have dichotomous thinking. The medical does not nullify the spiritual. Whatever happened to sin? Did we explain it away medically?

7   Personal and political advancement in both the secular and Christian world may, at times, be impeded by taking a stand against a particular sin. Power is an intimidating foe. How many would cross the line at the Alamo today? Whatever happened to sin? Did politics play an intimidating role?

Of the three big sins of "lust of the flesh," "lust of the eyes," and "the pride of life," which one may be the most difficult to recognize? Of the three big sins, on which one did Christ seem to focus with the religious leaders of his day? Of the three big sins, which one may have insidiously infiltrated Christianity today? Of the three big sins, which one may hold latent danger for most of us if God chooses to bless us?

Pride and humility are somewhat opposites. Apparently God likes humility. "Now the man Moses was very humble, more than all men who were on the face of the earth" (Num. 12:3 NKJV). How many Christian leaders do you know who are humble in their behavior, responses, and demeanor? How many Christian schools do you know that promote humility over academics? How many Christian boards do you know that are organized around humility? Certainly we all know some, but does a problem exist with the sin of pride? Whatever happened to sin? Is there one aspect that has gone under cover?

The draw of sin is great and has many pleasures—lust of the flesh, lust of the eyes, and the pride of life (1 John 2:16). I was talking recently to a once very godly friend—steeped in the Scriptures and the dangers of sin. We had often given talks together. Now he had left the wife of his youth and was living with a much younger woman. He said he had just fallen in love with her. The apostle Paul said, "For Demas has forsaken me, having loved this present world" (2 Tim. 4:11 NKJV). Whatever happened to sin? Did we fall in love with it?

God is a very patient God. Do we as a culture no longer fear him? Fear is not as good a motivator as love, I learned in psychiatry; but it is a motivator. Do we no longer believe sin will have consequences? When was the last time you saw someone truly fearful of God because of what he had done? Do we too quickly brush aside such verses as Galatians 6:7–8, "Do not be deceived, God is not mocked; for whatever a man sows, that he will also reap. For he who sows to his flesh will of the flesh reap corruption" (NKJV)? Whatever happened to sin? Have we preached love until we have forgotten fear?

No discussion of the demise of the concept of sin would be complete without a reference to the mastermind behind the demise. Although I had known the concepts in general for years, in seminary three factors were summarized for me that I believe are major factors in the demise of the concept of sin. They are found in 1 John 2:14–16. That passage speaks of "the evil one" (Satan), "the world," and "the flesh." The "flesh" is that sinful part of our personality that combines with the "world system" headed by the "evil one" to lead us astray. Whatever happened to sin? Have we been outwitted by a mastermind?

Whatever happened to sin? It was certainly talked about when I was a child. Many may remember T. H. Fillmore's hymn:

> I am resolved no longer to linger,
> Charmed by the world's delights;
> Things that are higher, things that are nobler,
> These have allured my sight.

> I am resolved to go to the Savior,
> Leaving my sins and strife;

He is the true one, he is the just one,
He hath the words of life.

Man without Christ is lost, incomplete, depraved, under attack, and sinful. For the Christian counselor to be effective, he must be attuned to all of these principles in his approach.

Summary Questions for Chapter 1

1. Name six reasons Christian counseling is unique.	1. The Bible is the final standard of authority. 2. It depends on the power of the Holy Spirit in the Christian. 3. It deals with all time factors in a problem a person might be facing (past, present, and future). 4. It is based on God's love. 5. It has universal application to all people of all cultures. 6. It deals with all components of man (physical, psychological, and spiritual).
2. Name five basic principles essential to Christian counseling.	1. Man without Christ is lost. 2. Man without Christ is incomplete. 3. Man is depraved. 4. Man is under spiritual attack. 5. Man is sinful.

2

The Parts of Man and Christian Counseling

The Bible speaks of the importance of the parts of man. There is a good and strikingly close correlation between the description given in the Bible and that formulated from observations and theories in psychiatry. However, there are differences. The Bible and secular theorists are alike in that they describe the struggles between the parts of man. For example, psychoanalysis describes a struggle between the drives in man (*id*) and his conscience (*superego*). The Bible describes the struggle between carnal desires and the Holy Spirit in a Christian. However, the descriptions are different in that one is a theory and pertains to man without Christ, and the other is a fact and pertains to the Christian.

The secular counselor has ignored the spiritual aspect of man. How can a part of the whole be ignored? Can denial be used to ignore a part of man on the assumption that it should not be dealt with by the counselor? Can man be fractionated and each part dealt with separately?

Theologians have long debated whether man is dichotomous (consisting of two parts) or trichotomous (consisting of three parts). Others have written extensively about these parts, but the following is a brief review.

Man desires to be dealt with as a whole. The Bible describes the whole man as consisting of a body, soul, and spirit. Furthermore, it describes in detail the parts of these entities. The Bible's account of the parts of man is the most accurate ever given. It is based on the words of the One who made man—God himself. An understanding of these parts of man is basic to sound counseling. Confusion of the functions of one part with functions of another has resulted in much misunderstanding through the years.

Man Consists of a Body, Soul, and Spirit

In 1 Thessalonians 5:23, the following is recorded: "Now may the God of peace Himself sanctify you entirely; and may your spirit and soul and body be preserved complete, without blame at the coming of our Lord Jesus Christ" (NASB). This is a very significant verse, for it refers to three distinct and separate parts of man. The distinction is not unlike that heard in secular areas where man in totality is referred to as spirit, soul, and body. The reference is to the spiritual aspect of man, the psychological aspect of man, and, finally, the physical aspect. In the above verse, each part is considered separately, and each has different functions; yet they must complement to make a whole.

The whole of man is again described in a very early portion of Scripture. In Genesis 2:7, the following is recorded: "Then the LORD God formed man of dust from the ground (Hebrew word for body is *basar*) (Vine, 1985, p. 83), and breathed into his nostrils the breath of life (Hebrew word *neshamah*, meaning the human spirit, is used here); and man became a living being (can also be translated "soul"—Hebrew word for soul here is *nephesh*) (Vine, 1985, p. 237)" (NASB). Thus, God combined body plus spirit to form the soul.

Soul or Psyche

The Greek word for soul is *psyche* (Vine, 1985, p. 588). It has various meanings in the New Testament, and theologians Chafer, Hodge, Vine, and Strong differ on whether it should be considered a different entity from spirit.

The word *soul* is most often used as a synonym for the person—the self. In fact, translators have often translated the word *soul* as "self." Hence, Matthew 16:26 and Luke 9:25 have very similar wording, but one passage records the word *soul* and the other records the word *self*. Thus, the soul is the *self*—the person. An individual composed of spiritual capacities, plus genetic potentials, results in a unique personality, *self* or *soul*. With his body man is in contact with the physical world around him. With his spirit man has the potential of being in contact with the inner or spiritual. In between the two resides the soul, with its psychological and mental functions.

The soul—the psychological. The soul is the psychological aspect of man. Psychiatrists and psychologists have focused the thrust of their endeavors on this aspect of man. The hope has been to help individuals with confused minds, weak wills, and labile emotions. The Bible focuses on these three functions of the soul. In Job 6:7 and Job 7:15, reference is made to the ability of the soul to choose (the will). In Psalm 139:14 and Proverbs 19:2, reference is made to the intellectual or knowing aspect of the soul (the mind). Finally, in 2 Samuel 5:8 and Song of Solomon 1:7, reference is made to "emotions" as a function of the soul.

A Christian's problems may be manifested through any one of the parts of the soul. He may be very emotional, and these emotions can spring from a purely psychological base rather than a spiritual base. Other Christians may become angry easily or develop bitterness quickly. In addition, a Christian's problem may be manifested through his will. He may identify with the apostle Paul's statement, "I do the very thing I do not want to do" (Rom. 7:16 NASB). Lastly, the Christian's problem may manifest in his intellect—his mind. He may, like the Pharisees, know every "jot and tittle" of the law and yet be miserable. He fails to recognize that the mind alone lies in the psychological aspect of man and not the spiritual.

The soul is a major area of attack by Satan. For an immature Christian, Satan might attack through a carnal expression of the body, such as lust-provoking sights that the eyes behold. However, for a more mature Christian, he might focus the temptation a step deeper into the makeup of man and infect his soul—his mind, emotions, or will. Satan throws mental "darts" (see Eph. 6:16 KJV) figuratively, in an attempt to establish obsessions ("strongholds") and delusions ("imaginations") in the mind of a Christian (see 2 Cor. 10:4–5 KJV). Thus, Christians do have mental problems; a significant percentage of patients we treat are Christians.

The Christian with mental problems may, just like the non-Christian, work at a disadvantage to try to handle his problems. If he is depending on his own ability, his own objectivity, or his own logic, he may improve temporarily. Yet he labors at a distinct disadvantage.

The Spirit or Pneuma

This leads to a discussion of the innermost aspect of man—the *spirit*. The *spirit* is the supernatural part of man given by God at birth. It is not to be equated with the Holy Spirit of God, received by Christians at the time of conversion. The term *spirit* is used to denote several functions in the Bible.

Functions of the Spirit. The following are two key functions of the *spirit*. The first is that the *spirit* is the organ for communion with God. Christ stated, "But an hour is coming, and now is, when the true worshipers shall worship the Father in spirit and truth; for such people the Father seeks to be His worshipers" (John 4:23 NASB). This is why a person can intellectually know all about Christ and yet never experience the joy of a personal relationship with him.

When a person comes to recognize that Christ was the Son of God—that he died on the cross for his sins, that he rose from the grave and thus was victorious over death—forsakes his own futile efforts to be righteous, and accepts the righteousness of God, Jesus Christ, then he becomes a Christian. When a person believes in Christ or receives him as his Savior, then the Holy Spirit comes to indwell that person, that person's human *spirit* (see John 3:6 NASB).

Another important function of the spirit is perception and insight. This perception comes from deep within and is independent of mental reasoning. In Mark 2:8 an instance is recorded when the scribes were reasoning but Christ was perceiving in his spirit. What a contrast! How can one determine if an impression is from the spirit or just from the mind (soul)? One way is through a living knowledge of the Word of God: "For the word of God is living and active and sharper than any two-edged sword, and piercing as far as the division of soul and spirit, of both joints and marrow, and able to judge the thoughts and intentions of the heart" (Heb. 4:12 NASB).

The above paragraph discusses the conscience as one function of the Holy Spirit. However, the Christian should remember that the Holy Spirit only makes up one factor of the conscience in a Christian and not the whole conscience. The other factors contributing to the conscience of the Christian are the early parental teachings that were both mentally healthy and not mentally healthy (either too rigid or not strict enough). When one understands that one of three factors influencing the conscience of the Christian can be unhealthy, he can understand why a

Christian as well as a non-Christian can have psychological problems in his conscience. The Holy Spirit's convictions are never unhealthy; neither are certain aspects of early parental teachings. However, the unhealthy aspects of early parental teachings do produce problems. For example, parents who are extremely strict, dominating, or legalistic produce a child with a conscience that is always condemning him and that he can never please. Of course, the other extreme (parents who are not strict enough) is equally harmful.

Why Christians Have Emotional Problems

The reasons Christians have emotional problems are many. However, there is one factor about the Christian we wish to emphasize. Many problems could be avoided for the Christian if he just lived a life constantly as Christ wanted him to live. He would avoid doing many things that cause guilt, anxiety, and stress. Thus, the following question arises: If Christians have a new life and power within them at the time of conversion, why do they continue to have mental and emotional problems? One reason is that the mind is a part of the soul, not the spirit. The soul does not become new or have any change at the time of conversion; the spirit does. Only after a person has spent time in the Word of God, in prayer, and in fellowship is the mind renewed in accordance with the will of God (see Rom. 12:1). After receiving Christ, a person will sin periodically with vain thoughts and actions because he chooses, unfortunately, to yield his soul to the authority not of the Holy Spirit, as God desires, but rather to the "flesh."

The Sinful Nature of Man—the Sarx

The Greek word for flesh is *sarx* (Vine, 1985, p. 242). *Sarx* has a variety of meanings in the New Testament. Among these are "the source of sin in human nature" (see 1 John 2:16), "the weaker element of an individual" (see Rom. 8:39), and "the carnal element in the Christian" (see Gal. 5:17). The Christian may be thrown into a dilemma as both the flesh and the Spirit compete for control. "For the flesh sets its desire against the Spirit, and the Spirit against the flesh; for these are in opposition to one another" (Gal. 5:17 NASB).

Thus, a Christian is very complex in his makeup. Just as psychiatry has surmised, conflict between internal parts can produce anxiety. One of the best examples of the interrelation between the parts of man in producing emotional stress was expressed by Paul:

> For I know that nothing good dwells in me, that is, in my flesh; for the will is present in me, but the doing of the good is not. For the good that I want, I do not do, but I practice the very evil that I do not want. But if I am doing the very thing I do not want, I am no longer the one doing it, but sin which dwells in me. I find then the principle that evil is present in me, the one who wants to do good. For I joyfully concur with the law of God in the inner man, but I see a different law in the members of my body, waging war against the law of my mind, and making me a prisoner of the law of sin which is in my members. Wretched man that I am! Who will set me free from the body of this death? Thanks be to God through Jesus Christ our Lord! So then, on the one hand I myself with my mind am serving the law of God, but on the other, with my flesh the law of sin.

Therefore there is now no condemnation for those who are in Christ Jesus. For the law of the Spirit of life in Christ Jesus has set you free from the law of sin and of death (Rom. 7:18–8:2 NASB).

Conclusion: Dichotomous vs. Trichotomous

According to the *American College Dictionary*, *dichotomous* is defined as "divided or dividing into two parts," material and immaterial. *Trichotomous* is defined as being divided into three parts: "The three-part division of man into body, spirit and soul."

Vine's Complete Expository Dictionary of Old and New Testament Words (p. 589) says, "The language of Hebrews 4:2 suggests the extreme difficulty of distinguishing between the soul and the spirit alike in their nature and in their activities. Generally speaking, the spirit is the higher, the soul the lower element. The spirit may be recognized as the life principle bestowed on man by God, the soul as the resulting life constituted in the individual, the body being the material organism animated by soul and spirit."

"Body and soul are the constituents of the man according to Matthew 6:25; 10:28; Luke 12:20; Acts 20:10; body and spirit according to Luke 8:55; 1 Corinthians 5:3; 7:34; James 2:26. In Matthew 26:38 the emotions are associated with the soul, in John 13:21 with the spirit; cf. also Psalms 42:11 with 1 Kings 21:5. In Psalms 35:9 the soul rejoices in God, in Luke 1:47 in spirit" (Vine, 1985, p. 589).

"Apparently, then, the relationships may be thus summed up '*Soma*, body, and *pneuma*, spirit, may be separated, *pneuma* and *psuche*, soul, can only be distinguished'" (Vine, 1985, p. 589). Thus, whether a person is dichotomous or trichotomous does not negate the need to deal with the whole person—spirit, soul, and body. Both usually agree that they are not the same, and both should be dealt with in counseling.

Summary Questions for Chapter 2

Although theologians disagree on the exact parts of man with a dichotomous view versus trichotomous view, they do agree that certain words such as spirit, soul, body are present (1 Thess. 5:23). Name three areas the Christian counselor must be aware of.	1. Spiritual issues. 2. Issues of the mind, emotions, and will. 3. Physical problems.

3

An Analysis of the Biblical Word *Counsel*

The Balance Needed in Christian Counseling

Just as balance is the key to both spiritual and emotional maturity, so is balance the key to successful Christian counseling. For example, Jesus Christ had tremendous balance. He knew when to be directive and when to help others gain insight through parables (John 2). He knew when to focus on the present without excluding the past (John 4). He knew when to focus on the spiritual aspect of man but not neglect the physical and psychological aspects (John 5).

The apostle Paul also had emotional and spiritual balance. In 1 Thessalonians 5:14, Paul recorded the balance that is needed in counseling. I first noted this verse while I was in my residency training in psychiatry. As I was studying one day and attempting to integrate my newly found psychiatric knowledge with Scripture, my eyes fell on this verse, "We urge you, brethren, admonish the unruly, encourage the fainthearted, help the weak, be patient with everyone" (1 Thess. 5:14 NASB).

As we read the verse, we note that everyone was not counseled in the same manner. Some were admonished, or in present-day terminology, they were treated with a matter-of-fact approach. Some were encouraged, an approach that makes us think of a psychiatric approach known as "active friendliness." And yet others were to be helped in a supportive, friendly manner. All were to be treated with patience.

Thus, psychiatrically and biblically, it becomes evident that everyone should not be counseled in the same way. At times a counselor should be confronting, at other times not. An active, friendly approach would help some people, while others would only become worse with this approach. In short, one type of counseling will not work with all people.

Certainly the Scriptures are the basis for the truths in counseling, but the personal application of these truths will vary with the particular need of the counselee. It is part of the role of the effective counselor to know when to be "gentle as a lamb" or "shrewd as a serpent" in his or her approach.

Five Greek Verbs on Counseling

There are five variations of biblical verbs on counseling. They are *parakaleo, noutheteo, para-mutheomai, antechomai,* and *makrothumeo.* These five Greek verbs are used in 1 Thessalonians 5:14 mentioned above.

The first verb is *parakaleo.* Paul used this counseling verb himself as he began his statement on the different types of counseling. It means "to beseech or exhort, encourage or comfort" (Vine, 1985, p. 111). It is used in a milder sense than the next verb, which means "to admonish." In the original Greek text, this next verb is found in Romans 12:1; 2 Corinthians 1:4; and Romans 15:30 quoted respectively below.

> I beseech you therefore, brethren, by the mercies of God, that ye present your bodies a living sacrifice, holy, acceptable unto God, which is your reasonable service (Rom. 12:1 KJV).

> Who comforteth us in all our tribulation, that we may be able to comfort them which are in any trouble, by the comfort wherewith we ourselves are comforted of God (2 Cor. 1:4 KJV).

> Now I beseech you, brethren, for the Lord Jesus Christ's sake, and for the love of the Spirit, that ye strive together with me in your prayers to God for me (Rom. 15:30 KJV).

Parakaleo is an active verb. It is the verb on which Paul Morris bases his counseling known as love therapy.

The next Greek verb is *noutheteo.* This verb can be used in a broad context in counseling, but in the New Testament it usually means "to put in mind, to warn, and to confront" (Vine, 1985, p. 666). It is intended to produce a change in lifestyle. One especially admonishes the unruly, the undisciplined, or the impulsive, but we also admonish one another. This verb appears in these verses:

> And concerning you, my brethren, I myself also am convinced that you yourselves are full of goodness, filled with all knowledge, and able also to admonish one another (Rom. 15:14 NASB).

I am not writing this to shame you, but to warn you, as my dear children (1 Cor. 4:14 NIV).

Let the word of Christ richly dwell within you, with all wisdom teaching and admonishing one another with psalms and hymns and spiritual songs, singing with thankfulness in your hearts to God (Col. 3:16 NASB).

Noutheteo is also an active verb. It is the verb on which Jay Adams bases his "nouthetic counseling."

The third counseling verb is *paramutheomai*. It means "to have a positive attitude, to cheer up, to encourage" (Vine, 1985, p. 198). One encourages the fainthearted or discouraged. It is found in the original Greek text as follows, "Just as you know how we were exhorting and encouraging and imploring each one of you as a father would his own children" (1 Thess. 2:11 NASB).

The fourth counseling verb is *antechomai*. It means "to be available, to cling to, to hold fast, to take an interest in, to hold up spiritually or emotionally, to support" (Vine, 1985, p. 306). It is a passive verb.

The fifth Greek verb is *makrothumeo*. It means "to be patient" or "to have persistence" (Vine, 1985, p. 463). It is found in Matthew 18:26, 29; James 5:7; and Hebrews 6:15. It is also a passive verb.

Thus, there is not just one biblical verb on counseling in the New Testament; there are several. This shows that a person needs balance in his counseling approach. Christian counseling is unique in its ability to provide this balance.

Six Hebrew Words on Counsel

In the Old Testament there are also several Hebrew words pertaining to counsel:

Dabar. The "counsel of Balaam" (Num. 31:16 KJV) refers to advice (Strong, 1984, p. 29).

Ya'ats. "As he was talking with him, the king said to him, "Have we appointed you a royal counselor?" (2 Chron. 25:16a NASB). Here again counsel pertains to advice and direction (Strong, 1984, p. 50).

Sod. David's reference to the "sweet counsel" (Ps. 55:14 KJV) he had received from a former friend carries the connotation of fellowship and sharing (Strong, 1984, p. 82).

'eta. That Daniel answered Arioch "with counsel" (Dan. 2:14 KJV) implies that he responded with discretion (Strong, 1984, p. 87).

'etsah. Israel's lack "in counsel" (Deut. 32:28 NASB) suggests a lack of advice (Strong, 1984, p. 90).

yasad. "The rulers take counsel together" (Ps. 2:2 KJV) means that they sit down together for a period of mutual consultation, deliberation, and instruction (Strong, 1984, p. 50).

That the Bible uses several words for counsel seems to imply that different approaches are suitable for different counseling situations.

Evaluation of Various Bible Passages in Regard to Counseling

Various biblical passages indicate different approaches to individuals. There are times to be direct (Prov. 27:5–6); there are times to be indirect (Nathan with David in 2 Sam. 12:1–25); there are times to be gentle (Christ with the little children), and there are times to confront strongly (Christ with the Pharisees); there is a time to speak and a time to listen (Eccles. 3:7).

Conclusion

Whether one evaluates Greek verbs on counsel, Hebrew words on counsel, or just the Bible in various passages, the conclusion is the same. There is not just one approach to Christian counseling. Each person must be met at his or her point of need.

Summary Questions for Chapter 3

1. Name five different Greek verbs on counseling taken from one verse (1 Thess. 5:14).	1. *parakaleo* 2. *noutheteo* 3. *paramutheomai* 4. *antechomai* 5. *makrothumeo*
2. Name six different Hebrew words on counseling.	1. *Dabar* 2. *Ya'ats* 3. *Sowd* 4. *'eta* 5. *'etsah* 6. *yasadsad*
3. In the light of the above, is one approach or technique applicable to all people in all situations?	No.

4

Helping the Client Grow in Christ and Thus Overcome Many Problems

The most important decision that a person will ever make is whether to accept Christ. The second most important decision is whether one will avail himself of the tools which will enable him or her to grow in Christ. One of the greatest mistakes Christian counselors make is to focus mostly on the problems while failing to emphasize these strong basics that allow people ultimately to overcome their problems. Much heartache can be averted by growth in Christ. Here are some supremely powerful tools. The Christian counselor may wish to encourage the client just to try them for one month but give this warning: life may never be the same.

Christianity Is Having a Relationship with Christ

A person starts a relationship with Christ through faith or belief. Many people will reflect back on a prayer similar to the following when they came to know Christ:

- "I realize I am a sinner. I have done things sinful and wrong" ("For all have sinned, and come short of the glory of God" Rom. 3:23 KJV).
- "I realize that your Son Christ died on a cross in payment for my sins" ("For the wages of sin is death; but the gift of God is eternal life through Jesus Christ our Lord" Rom. 6:23 KJV).
- "I am at this moment accepting his death on the cross as payment for my sins. I receive him as my Savior" ("But as many as received him, to them gave he power to become the sons of God, even to them that believe on his name" John 1:12 KJV).

If one has believed as above, he has a relationship with God (John 1:12); he has entered a new family (Eph. 3:15); he is a new creation (2 Cor. 5:17); he has an unbelievable new power; he will spend an eternity with God (1 John 5:11–12); he is a Christian.

Six Encouragements to the New (or Old) Christian

The Christian has the best encouragement in the world.

He can be assured that he is, indeed, a Christian ("All that the Father giveth me shall come to me; and him that cometh to me I will in no wise cast out," John 6:37 KJV) and will have eternal life ("And this is the record, that God hath given to us eternal life, and this life is in his Son. He that hath the Son has life; and he that hath not the Son of God hath not life," 1 John 5:11–12 KJV).

He can be assured that he can have victory over temptations ("Hitherto have ye asked nothing in my name: ask, and ye shall receive, that your joy may be full," John 16:24 KJV).

He can be assured that he can have victory over temptations ("There hath no temptation taken you but such as is common to man: but God is faithful, who will not suffer you to be tempted above that ye are able; but will with the temptation also make a way to escape, that ye may be able to bear it," 1 Cor. 10:13 KJV).

He can be assured of guidance from God ("Trust in the LORD with all thine heart; and lean not unto thine own understanding. In all thy ways acknowledge him, and he shall direct thy paths," Prov. 3:5–6 KJV).

He can be assured of forgiveness when he does sin and fall ("If we confess our sins, he is faithful and just to forgive us our sins, and to cleanse us from all unrighteousness," 1 John 1:9 KJV).

He can be assured that God will help him ("I can do all things through Christ which strengtheneth me," Phil. 4:13 KJV; "He said unto me, My grace is sufficient for thee: for my strength is made perfect in weakness. Most gladly therefore will I rather glory in my infirmities, that the power of Christ may rest upon me," 2 Cor. 12:9 KJV). The new Christian is not alone.

Getting to Know Christ—the Daily Quiet Time—a Major Tool

Probably less than ten percent of Christians have a daily quiet time. Yet one very important principle in maturing in Christ is simply to spend a little time with God daily in what has been called a daily quiet time ("And in the morning, rising up a great while before day, he went out, and departed into a solitary place, and there prayed," Mark 1:35 KJV; "And the LORD spake unto Moses face to face, as a man speaketh unto his friend," Exod. 33:11a KJV). One might want to start with a minimum of five minutes per day (two and one-half minutes in prayer and two and one-half minutes in the Bible).

Prayer: The word *pray* has been used as an acrostic to suggest how one might pray.

Praise: Tell God how much you appreciate him. He is holy and deserves our worship ("And he said, Draw not nigh hither: put off thy shoes from off thy feet, for the place whereon thou standest is holy ground," Exod. 3:5 KJV).

Request: Ask God for needs (personal, family, friends, health, finances, missionaries, those who don't know Christ, etc.). ("Hear my prayer, O LORD, give ear to my supplications: in thy faithfulness answer me," Ps. 143:1 KJV.) Ask him for his presence that day.

Ask for forgiveness of sin: Agree with God regarding sins of omission (not doing the things one should do) and commission (doing the things one should not do). Ask for forgiveness ("If I regard iniquity in my heart, the Lord will not hear me," Ps. 66:18 KJV).

Your thanks of past answered prayer. Thank God for all of his blessings and answered prayer ("In every thing give thanks: for this is the will of God in Christ Jesus concerning you," 1 Thess. 5:18 KJV).

The two and one-half minutes in God's Word might be spent reading or memorizing a specific verse that would encourage people in their time of need (see following list).

Summary

Counselors may wish to avail themselves of this helpful tool for a commitment right now of five minutes per day. It is the best time ever spent. Though less than ten percent of all Christians have a daily quiet time, it may represent the heart of the Christian life.

The Bible Gives Practical Answers to Problems We Face

1. Overcoming depression	Ps. 43:5	19. Friendship	Eccles. 4:9–10
2. Overcoming anxiety	Phil. 4:6–8	20. Bold requests	1 Chron. 4:10
3. Overcoming loneliness	Heb. 3:5	21. Joy of God's Word	Luke 24:32
4. Overcoming anger	Eph. 4:31–32	22. Power of God's Word	Heb. 4:12
5. Overcoming lust	Job 31:1	23. The life of God's Word	John 6:63
6. Overcoming temptations	1 Cor. 1:3–4	24. Prosperity	Ps. 1:2–3
7. Overcoming suffering	2 Cor. 1:3–4	25. A new resource	2 Cor. 5:17
8. Overcoming fear	Ps. 34:4	26. Man's frailty	Rom. 7:18
9. Overcoming abandonment	Ps. 27:10	27. Care	1 Pet. 5:7
10. Overcoming worry	Matt. 6:33–34	28. Strength	Phil. 4:13
11. Overcoming trouble	2 Cor. 4:8–9	29. God's Spirit	Zech. 4:6b
12. Overcoming weakness	2 Cor. 12:9	30. Thought of peace	Jer. 29:11
13. Overcoming trials	Rom. 8:28	31. Failing	Ps. 37:23–24
14. Overcoming guilt	1 John 1:9	32. Drawing closer to God	Ps. 42:1
15. Overcoming faintness	Heb. 12:1–3	33. The impossible	Gen. 18:14a
16. Doing your part	Prov. 21:31	34. Assurance of vindication	Rom. 12:19
17. Focusing on behavior	Gen. 4:6–7	35. Focus on the future	John 14:1–3
18. Focusing on thinking	Phil. 4:8	36. Your favorite verse	

Six Ways to Grow in Christ

God's Word

"Wherewithal shall a young man cleanse his way? by taking heed thereto according to thy word. . . . Thy word have I hid in mine heart, that I might not sin against thee" (Ps. 119:9, 11 KJV).

One can take in God's Word through hearing, reading, studying (Acts 17:1–3), meditating (Ps. 1:2–3), and memorizing (Ps. 119:9–11). A person retains perhaps ten percent that is heard, twenty percent that is read, thirty percent that is studied, forty percent that is meditated upon, but one hundred percent that is truly memorized with meditation.

Prayer

"Let us therefore come boldly unto the throne of grace, that we may obtain mercy, and find grace to help in time of need" (Heb. 4:16 KJV). Prayer is conversation with God. One may wish to keep a personal prayer journal to record prayer requests and to note when God answers. It can be a powerful reminder of God's care for you.

Fellowship

"Not forsaking the assembling of ourselves together, as the manner of some is; but exhorting one another: and so much the more, as ye see the day approaching" (Heb. 10:25 KJV). Fellowship comes from the Greek word *koinonia*, which means "sharing in common" (Vine, 1985, p. 233). We can share through love and concern (1 John 4:21), guidance (Gal. 6:1), and prayers (James 5:16). It involves both living and receiving. It sharpens us (Prov. 27:17), helps prevent our failing (Eccles. 4:9–10), and encourages us (Heb. 10:25). One might wish to ask God specifically to bring individuals into his or her life for encouragement. Many churches now have small groups for fellowship and to help meet individual needs.

Witnessing

"For I delivered unto you first of all that which I also received, how that Christ died for our sins according to the scriptures; and that he was buried, and that he rose again the third day according to the scriptures" (1 Cor. 15:3–4 KJV). Telling others about Christ can also help us to grow in Christ. When sharing one's testimony, it helps to make it personal, short, and Christ centered. It may be helpful to write out a few key verses.

Focusing on Christ

"I am crucified with Christ: nevertheless I live; yet not I, but Christ liveth in me: and the life which I now life in the flesh I live by the faith of the Son of God, who loved me, and gave himself for me" (Gal. 2:20 KJV). Growth in Christ is centered around an emphasis on Christ. In fact, the Christian life is an impossible life to live without a reliance upon a close, wonderful, personal relationship with Christ.

Obedience to Christ

The law of the LORD is perfect, converting the soul: the testimony of the LORD is sure, making wise the simple. The statutes of the LORD are right, rejoicing the heart: the commandment of the LORD is pure, enlightening the eyes. The fear of the LORD is clean, enduring for ever: the judgments of the LORD are true and righteous all together. More to be desired are they than gold, yea, than much fine gold: sweeter also than honey and the honeycomb. Moreover by them is thy servant warned: and in keeping of them there is great reward (Ps. 19:7–11 KJV).

The Word of God puts a great emphasis on what we do—our obedience. *What* we do in obedience may be even more important than *why* we take certain actions. The *what* is more concrete and more open to intervention on our part. In short, it offers more immediate results and hope.

Conclusion

A Christian is simply a person who has trusted Christ as his or her Savior. With the acceptance of Christ, one became a new creature (2 Cor. 5:17), and the wonderful new resource of the Holy Spirit is available to help overcome problems everyone faces. Maturing in Christ is possible through God's Word, prayer, fellowship, witnessing, and obedience. A daily quiet time can be of great help.

Summary Questions for Chapter 4

1. Give three Bible verses that are used to share the gospel.	1. Romans 3:23: The fact of sin. 2. Romans 6:23: The penalty of sin. 3. John 1:12: The receiving of Christ.
2. Name five encouragements of biblical facts that the new Christian can be assured of in his or her new life in Christ.	1. He/she is saved (John 6:37). 2. He/she can have victory over temptation (1 Cor. 10:13). 3. He/she can have guidance (Prov. 3:5–6). 4. He/she can be assured of forgiveness (1 John 1:9). 5. He/she can be assured God will help in time of need (Phil. 4:13).
3. Name seven ways the Christian can grow in Christ and thus avoid many emotional problems.	1. The daily quiet time. 2. God's Word. 3. Prayer. 4. Fellowship with other Christians. 5. Witnessing. 6. Focusing on Christ. 7. Obedience to Christ.

5

An Analysis with Pragmatic Solutions for Four of the Most Common Emotions in Counseling

Do certain emotions appear more than others in Christian counseling? The answer is *yes,* and the following deals with four of the most common emotions (anxiety, depression, anger, and guilt). Much has been written in the secular world about each of these, but little has been written on these from a strong biblical evaluation. Here are the biblical evaluations. After all, the Bible is the Christian counselor's guide.

An Analysis of Anxiety

Anxiety is a painful or apprehensive uneasiness of mind usually over an impending or anticipated ill. There are often behavioral, psychological, and physiological manifestations.

Biblical Correlations and Integrations

Scripture indicates that some anxiety (a realistic concern as seen in such verses as 1 Cor. 12:25; 2 Cor. 11:28; and Phil. 2:20) is healthy. However, intense anxiety (fretting and worrying, as seen in such verses as Luke 8:14; Phil. 4:6; and 1 Pet. 5:7) is not healthy.

Both modern psychology and Scripture point out that anxiety exists in normal and abnormal amounts. Psychologists have long noted that people are more efficient and productive when they have a measure of anxiety. However, if the anxiety becomes intense, efficiency begins to decrease accordingly.

Methodology: Suggestions to Make to a Counselee Experiencing Anxiety

Determine to obey God: God commands us not to be anxious (Phil. 4:6).

Pray (Phil. 4:6): God told Daniel not to fear because God had heard his prayer from the time he first started praying, and he would answer (Dan. 10:12).

Realize that God can keep our minds safe as we obey him (Phil. 4:7).

Meditate on positive thoughts (Phil. 4:8): We have often encouraged people who catch themselves worrying to say, "Stop, relax; anxiety is a signal to relax, so relax." We then encourage them to go over and over a verse like Philippians 4:8. Anxiety is usually a signal to become more anxious; but by a simple technique of behavior modification, the brain can be conditioned to use anxiety as a signal to relax. There is no better place to find positive things to meditate on than the Scriptures (Ps. 34:4; 86:15; Prov. 1:33; 3:25–26; Isa. 40:28–31; Matt. 6:33–34; 11:28–29; John 10:27–28; 14:27; Heb. 4:15; 1 John 3:20; 4:10).

Realize there is a twofold responsibility (yours and Christ's) in doing anything. "I can do all things through Christ," the apostle Paul stated (Phil. 4:13 KJV). A person can overcome anxiety through Christ.

Realize that the grace of God is with you (2 Cor. 9:8; Phil. 4:23). The knowledge that one is never alone and that God's grace is always present can markedly decrease anxiety.

Cultivate the art of living one day at a time (Matt. 6:34). Probably 98 percent of the things we are anxious about never come true!

An Analysis of Guilt

Guilt is the feeling we have when we have committed an offense or done something wrong.

Biblical Correlations and Integrations

When we think of guilt, we almost automatically thinks of conscience as well. The functions of the conscience are ascribed to the "heart," which is a broad term used in connection with many aspects of intellectual, emotional, and moral life. Although the term *conscience* does not appear in the Old Testament, it does occur thirty-two times in the New Testament in the form of the Greek word *suneidesis*, which literally means "to know together with."

The New Testament makes use of three Greek words which can be translated "(to be) guilty": *hupodikos, opheilo,* and *enochos* (Vine, 1985, p. 285). They are generally used in a legal sense. Theological guilt is the realization that God's divine principles have been violated. This guilt is a normal and healthy reaction in keeping with the teaching of Scripture. It is important to note that theological guilt never involves a feeling of being rejected by God because of the offense, because God never rejects his children.

To feel guilty for having offended God's principles is healthy. But can the conscience always be used as a guide in such matters? Consider the implication of a verse like Hebrews 9:14: "The blood of Christ [will] . . . cleanse your conscience from dead works to serve the living God" (NASB). In this instance God stands against the conscience. The key question in determining whether the conscience is a reliable guide is, Does the conscience agree with the Word of God? When God convicts the conscience, he never goes against his Word.

In general, if there are no principles in the Word of God that relate to the matter in question, feelings of guilt are unnecessary. If such feelings do exist, the conscience may be overly strict. Guilt that drives a person to work all the time, and thus to pay little attention to his family and neglect daily devotions, is unnecessary. There is no text in Scripture that encourages guilt if a person does not work all the time. In fact, the principles of Scripture in this case would encourage less work in order that more time might be spent with God and the family.

The guilt we feel about matters not explicitly covered by scriptural principles is sometimes popularly referred to as "false guilt." Of course, it is debatable whether guilt is ever really false since it does in fact exist. Perhaps a more accurate term is "unnecessary guilt," although this term also has its drawbacks.

Precisely what is involved in false or unnecessary guilt? Several factors complicate the issue. For example, there is what Francis Schaeffer calls the "false tyranny of the conscience." That is, a person may continue to feel guilty even after confessing a known sin. But with confession God forgives, and guilt should be gone. There is also the matter of actions which are not wrong in themselves but that offend the overly strict conscience of weaker brothers. If a weaker brother commits such an act, he sins. Paul says regarding the eating of meat offered to idols, which does not in itself violate any of God's principles, "He who doubts is condemned if he eats, because his eating is not from faith; and whatever is not from faith is sin" (Rom. 14:23 NASB).

The issue is indeed complicated. For the purpose of this discussion, "false guilt" can be regarded as any guilt that is unnecessary in the sense that no specific principle in the Word of God has been violated. This in no way gives man license to do whatever he wishes. Just as many things are clearly encouraged in Scripture and should be done (e.g., letting the Word of God nourish us, 1 Pet. 2:2), other things are forbidden and should not be done (e.g., provoking our children to wrath, Col. 3:21). Naturally, God will convict us when we go against his Word or fail to live by it. Doing what he has forbidden will produce a healthy feeling of guilt.

Finally, what is true guilt? True guilt is the conviction of wrongdoing when we have behaved in a manner that is clearly wrong according to Scripture (e.g., over moral sins; Gal. 5:19–21). This includes any behavior that offends a weaker brother (1 Cor. 8, etc.). Such behavior will produce a conviction of guilt. The knowledge that God loves and accepts us, but that we have offended him, is healthy in this case.

Methodology: Suggestions to Make to a Counselee Experiencing Guilt

Confess true guilt (1 John 1:9) in order to restore fellowship with God and relieve any physical symptoms that may have been caused by the guilt (Ps. 32:3–5).

Deal with false and unnecessary guilt by being reeducated according to the Word of God. This guilt may have arisen from rigid rules in childhood that prevented development of a proper understanding of God's grace. It is essential to realize that man is unconditionally accepted (no performance necessary) by God once he trusts Christ. The heavenly Father will never reject him. Man must recognize that he is of great worth to God and has the ability to do whatever God wants him to do.

An Analysis of Anger

Anger is an emotional reaction of extreme displeasure. It often involves antagonism. Related terms include ire, rage, fury, indignation, and wrath.

Biblical Correlations and Integrations

That anger is a far-too-common emotion is suggested by the fact that the term (including its cognates) occurs 275 times in the King James translation. It is also instructive to note how many times related terms (and their cognates) appear:

abhor	43	grudge	5	strive	32
alienate	8	hate	207	variance	2
bitter	68	indignation	41	vengeance	44
despise	116	loathe	7	vex	52
enemy	375	malice	9	war	259
enmity	8	rage	25	wrath	200
fight	114	scorn	43	wroth	49
fury	70	strife	43		

Add to this the many scriptural examples of anger being carried out to the ultimate degree: Cain murdered his brother Abel, Moses killed an Egyptian slavemaster, Samson slaughtered a thousand Philistines, Christ was crucified.

In studying the emotion of anger, psychology concentrates on why man becomes angry and what he can do about it. By contrast, theology emphasizes man's very nature, which gives rise to his anger. The source of anger is man's old nature (he is ego centered; see Gen. 4:5–8; 27:42–45; 49:5–7; 1 Sam. 20:30; 1 Kings 21:4; 2 Kings 5:11; Matt. 2:16; Luke 4:28). But in addition to this negative, destructive emotion, there is also a righteous anger (Exod. 11:8; Lev. 10:16–17; Neh. 5:6–13; Ps. 97:10; Mark 3:5). It should be pointed out, then, that anger does not necessarily involve sin (Eph. 4:26). On the other hand, it is often a precursor of sin or a result of sin. Perhaps more important than the source is how anger is handled.

Methodology: Suggestions to Make to a Counselee Experiencing Anger

- Recognize the anger; be honest about its presence.
- Verbalize the anger to God, a friend, a counselor.
- Determine what figures in your past (parents, spouse, self, or others) are the real targets of your anger and choose to forgive them.
- Grow in Christ. The fruit of the Spirit (love, joy, peace, long-suffering, etc.) will work toward relieving anger and preventing anger in the future.

An Analysis of Depression

Depression is a disturbance of mood. It involves a happy-sad axis. A person who is experiencing depression may exhibit a sad affect, have painful thinking, develop a variety of physical symptoms, and be anxious. Depressed people feel blue and down and often experience a loss of interest or pleasure (anhedonia). Symptoms may include irritability, a disturbance of sleep or appetite, a loss of energy or fatigue, a decreased ability to make decisions, a diminished self-worth, a tendency to ruminate and even recurrent thoughts of not wanting to live, and various medical complaints for which no other medical cause can be found.

Depression affects everyone to some degree. Significant, medical-type depression affects over seventeen million Americans annually. The lifetime prevalence approaches a staggering twenty percent. It is more common than coronary heart disease and cancer combined (seventeen million people versus thirteen million people). It can be lethal (i.e., from suicide). The economic cost is high in the form of pain, family conflict, social withdrawal, work absenteeism, reduced productivity, unemployment, and alcohol and drug abuse. The economic cost for the treatment of depression is forty-four billion dollars annually, compared to forty-three billion dollars for coronary heart disease and cancer.

Depression remains undertreated (less than 25 percent receive an antidepressant); yet it is often more effectively treated than coronary heart disease and cancer. Left untreated, the probability of a more resistant type of depression may increase, with the potential for other lifelong implications. The treatment tools are significant today. The benefits for the individual may be great, and the cause for Christ may be immeasurable.

Biblical Correlations and Integrations

Scripture offers at least seven causes of depression.

1. A Homicidal Threat.

> And Ahab told Jezebel all that Elijah had done, also how he had executed all the prophets with the sword. Then Jezebel sent a messenger to Elijah, saying, "So let the gods do to me, and more also, if I do not make your life as the life of one of them by tomorrow about this time." And when he saw that, he arose and ran for his life, and went to Beersheba, which belongs to Judah, and left his servant there. But he himself went a day's journey into the wilderness, and came and sat down under a broom tree. And he prayed that he might die, and said, "It is enough! Now, Lord, take my life, for I am no better than my fathers!" (1 Kings 19:1–4 NKJV).

2. Losses.

> Now there was a day when his sons and daughters were eating and drinking wine in their oldest brother's house; and a messenger came to Job and said, "The oxen were plowing and the donkeys feeding beside them, when the

Sabeans raided them and took them away—indeed they have killed the servants with the edge of the sword; and I alone have escaped to tell you!" While he was still speaking, another also came and said, "The fire of God fell from heaven and burned up the sheep and the servants, and consumed them; and I alone have escaped to tell you!" While he was still speaking, another also came and said, "The Chaldeans formed three bands, raided the camels and took them away, yes, and killed the servants with the edge of the sword; and I alone have escaped to tell you!" While he was still speaking, another also came and said, "Your sons and daughters were eating and drinking wine in their oldest brother's house, and suddenly a great wind came from across the wilderness and struck the four corners of the house, and it fell on the young people, and they are dead; and I alone have escaped to tell you!" . . . After this Job opened his mouth and cursed the day of his birth. And Job spoke, and said: "May the day perish on which I was born, and the night in which it was said, 'A male child is conceived'" (Job 1:13–19, 3:1–3 NKJV).

3. Anger.

But it displeased Jonah exceedingly, and he became angry. So he prayed to the LORD, and said, "Ah, LORD, was not this what I said when I was still in my country? Therefore I fled previously to Tarshish; for I know that You are a gracious and merciful God, slow to anger and abundant in lovingkindness, One who relents from doing harm. Therefore now, O LORD, please take my life from me, for it is better for me to die than to live!" (Jon. 4:1–3 NKJV).

So the LORD said to Cain, "Why are you angry? And why has your countenance fallen? If you do well, will you not be accepted? And if you do not do well, sin lies at the door. And its desire is for you, but you should rule over it" (Gen. 4:6–7 NKJV).

4. A Wrong Perspective.

Truly God is good to Israel,
To such as are pure in heart.
But as for me, my feet had almost stumbled;
My steps had nearly slipped.
For I was envious of the boastful,
When I saw the prosperity of the wicked. . . .
When I thought how to understand this,
It was too painful for me—until I went into the sanctuary of God;
Then I understood their end" (Ps. 73:1–3, 16–17 NKJV).

5. A Lack of Faith.

> Why are you cast down, O my soul?
> And why are you disquieted within me?
> Hope in God, for I shall yet praise Him
> For the help of His countenance (Ps. 42:5 NKJV).

6. Rejection.

> Woe is me, my mother,
> That you have borne me,
> A man of strife and a man of contention to the whole earth!
> I have neither lent for interest,
> Nor have men lent to me for interest.
> Every one of them curses me (Jer. 15:10 NKJV).

7. Sin and Guilt.

> When I kept silent, my bones grew old
> Through my groaning all the day long.
> For day and night Your hand was heavy upon me;
> My vitality was turned into the drought of summer.
> I acknowledged my sin to You,
> And my iniquity I have not hidden.
> I said, "I will confess my transgressions to the LORD,"
> And You forgave the iniquity of my sin (Ps. 32:3–5 NKJV).

Methodology: Suggestions to Make to a Counselee Experiencing Depression

Seven men in the Bible dealt with depression. The Bible gives descriptions of several men who overcame depression and how they did it. The Bible also points to one man who did poorly with life, but God left us with a great lesson for overcoming a fallen countenance.

1. Refocus:

> Maschil, for the sons of Korah. "Why art thou cast down, O my soul? and why art thou disquieted within me? hope thou in God: for I shall yet praise him, who is the health of my countenance, and my God" (Ps. 42:11 KJV).

2. Change perspective:

> Asaph. "When I thought how to understand this,
> It was too painful for me—
> Until I went into the sanctuary of God;
> Then I understood their end" (Ps. 73:16–17 NKJV).

3. Attend to the physical and spiritual:

> Elijah. Sleep, supplements, God's Word, support. Then as he lay and slept under a broom tree, suddenly an angel touched him, and said to him, "Arise and eat." Then he looked, and there by his head was a cake baked on coals, and a jar of water. So he ate and drank, and lay down again. And the angel of the LORD came back the second time, and touched him, and said, "Arise and eat, because the journey is too great for you." So he arose, and ate and drank; and he went in the strength of that food forty days and forty nights as far as Horeb, the mountain of God. . . . And after the earthquake a fire, but the LORD was not in the fire; and after the fire a still small voice. . . . So he departed from there, and found Elisha, the son of Shaphat, who was plowing with twelve yoke of oxen before him, and he was with the twelfth. Then Elijah passed by him and threw his mantle on him (1 Kings 19:5–8, 12, 19 NKJV).

4. Repent:

> David. I acknowledged my sin to You,
> And my iniquity I have not hidden.
> I said, "I will confess my transgressions to the LORD,"
> And You forgave the iniquity of my sin (Ps. 32:5 NKJV).

5. Realize the big picture:

> Jonah. Then God said to Jonah, "Is it right for you to be angry about the plant?" And he said, "It is right for me to be angry, even to death!" But the LORD said, "You have had pity on the plant for which you have not labored, nor made it grow, which came up in a night and perished in a night. And should I not pity Nineveh, that great city, in which are more than one hundred and twenty thousand persons who cannot discern between their right hand and their left—and much livestock?" (Jon. 4:9–11 NKJV).

6. Grow close to God:

> Job. I have heard of You by the hearing of the ear,
> But now my eye sees You (Job 42:5 NKJV).

7. Enjoy God's Word:

> Jeremiah. Your words were found, and I ate them,
> And Your word was to me the joy and rejoicing of my heart (Jer. 15:16a NKJV).

8. Responsible behavior:

Cain did not succeed, but God pointed to the right direction with responsible behavior. "Then the LORD said to Cain, 'Why are you angry? And why has your countenance fallen? If you do well, will not your countenance be lifted up? And if you do not do well, sin is crouching at the door; and its desire is for you, but you must master it'" (Gen. 4:6–7 NASB).

Summary Questions for Chapter 5

1. True or False: Anxiety as a realistic concern is healthy, but intense anxiety is not healthy.	True, comparing Philippians 2:20, "For I have no one like-minded, who will sincerely care for your state" (NKJV), with Philippians 4:6, "Be anxious for nothing, but in everything by prayer and supplication, with thanksgiving, let your requests be made known to God" (NKJV).
2. Give an example from Scripture when guilt is unnecessary.	"For if our heart condemns us, God is greater than our heart, and knows all things" (1 John 3:20 NKJV).
3. Give a verse early in Scripture that is very applicable for depression and anger.	"So the LORD said to Cain, 'Why are you angry? And why has your countenance fallen? If you do well, will you not be accepted? And if you do not do well, sin lies at the door. And its desire is for you, but you should rule over it'" (Gen. 4:6–7 NKJV).
4. Give a Bible verse that points to an anger that occurs without sin.	"'Be angry, and do not sin': do not let the sun go down on your wrath" (Eph. 4:26 NKJV).

6

Seven Pragmatic and Biblical Steps in Christian Counseling

How Does One Actually Do Christian Counseling?

Are there pragmatic steps for Christian counseling that can be applied from the Bible? Here are seven.

Be Kind

Proverbs 19:22 states that what is desirable in a man is kindness. The apostle Paul in 1 Thessalonians 2:7 tells us that we should be "gentle." Furthermore, scientific research in evaluating different psychotherapeutic approaches found that it is not so much the specific approach used in therapy as it is the specific therapist. Therapists who exude warmth and genuineness and who are empathetic are the ones who get good results. Also, consider how warm the apostle Paul was toward those he was helping (Gal. 4:19; Phil. 1:7).

Showing kindness is one of the most important principles of all. A person cannot hear you if he does not sense that you care for him. In 1 Corinthians the issue is stated as follows:

If I speak in the tongues of men and of angels, but have not love, I am only a resounding gong or a clanging cymbal. If I have the gift of prophecy and can fathom all mysteries and all knowledge, and if I have a faith that can move mountains, but have not love, I am nothing. If I give all I possess to the poor and surrender my body to the flames, but have not love, I gain nothing. Love is patient, love is kind. It does not envy, it does not boast, it is not proud. It is not rude, it is not self-seeking, it is not easily angered, it keeps no record of wrongs.

Love does not delight in evil but rejoices with the truth. It always protects, always trusts, always hopes, always perseveres. Love never fails. But where there are prophecies, they will cease; where there are tongues, they will be stilled; where there is knowledge, it will pass away. For we know in part and we prophesy in part, but when perfection comes, the imperfect disappears. When I was a child, I talked like a child, I thought like a child, I reasoned like a child. When I became a man, I put childish ways behind me. Now we see but a poor reflection as in a mirror; then we shall see face to face. Now I know in part; then I shall know fully, even as I am fully known. And now these three remain: faith, hope and love. But the greatest of these is love (1 Cor. 13:1–13 NIV).

Start with Behavior

An important starting point in therapy is a focus on behavior. While therapy certainly involves much more, this is nonetheless an important step. When Solomon, the wisest man who ever lived (other than Christ), was giving the essence of the responsibility of man, one of his two areas of recommendation had to do with behavior (Eccles. 2:13). The Scriptures are replete with emphases on behavior, from Genesis 4:6–7 throughout the rest of the Bible. The importance is magnified in verses such as Philippians 2:13, "For it is God which worketh in you both to will and to do of his good pleasure" (KJV), and in Philippians 4:13, "I can do all things through Christ which strengtheneth me" (KJV), as well as through the entire Book of James. I did a study of the books of the Bible. The emphasis is clearly on behavior.

Also, it is important to realize that although feelings are extremely important and should be listened to, most individuals have very little direct control over changing their feelings. In my years of practice, I have rarely seen a depressed person feel sad and choose immediately to feel happy. What we do have control over, however, is behavior. We choose what time we get up, who we talk with during the day, whether we exercise, whether we read and study the Scriptures, and so on. We have maximum control over what we do. All of us tend to follow a cycle where feelings follow behavior and behavior follows feelings. Let's interrupt where we have control—in the area of behavior.

We often start by having patients make a specific behavioral plan involving daily quiet time, weekly exercise programs, daily social contact, and avoiding specific sinful behaviors. Helping to redirect behavior also gives the new client a feeling of direction and control. Just to be listened to and then left to oneself without clear guidelines is often very disturbing for the counselee.

Help the Counselee Gain Insight

King David stated this principle clearly in Psalm 139:23–24, "Search me, O God, and know my heart: try me, and know my thoughts: And see if there be any wicked way in me, and lead me in the way everlasting" (KJV). The apostle Paul wrote his epistles to educate the churches and to help them gain insight into their behavior. If you evaluate it from a scientific standpoint, then you would come to this conclusion: A person cannot change if he does not know the problem.

If a religious leader thinks his demanding perfectionism or his unwarranted suspicions and paranoia come from godliness, how can he change? If a husband thinks his use of Ephesians 5:22 to make his wife more submissive is based on godliness, when he in reality may be very selfish, how can he change?

If a Christian leader's relentless drive comes from past issues, and he is really addicted to an excessive work schedule in the cloak of having a successful ministry for Christ, how can he change?

Indeed, knowing how the past affects the present and creates sinful defense mechanisms, which turn into ungodly transference issues and then into inappropriate injunctions, is an invaluable tool.

Help with the Resolution of Feelings

Feelings are important as demonstrated by Hebrews 4:16: "Let us therefore come boldly unto the throne of grace, that we may obtain mercy, and find grace to help in time of need" (KJV). Hurt feelings and bitterness not dealt with become like a festering sore. When lancing the sore, pain is elicited, but if the sore is not lanced, disease results. Counselees do need to be honest about their feelings. To deny feelings does not make them go away. God knows everything; he knows how we feel. Years of repressing the feelings resulting from a history of abuse in early life does not make them go away. Feelings are recorded in biochemical pathways of the brain, and they cannot be simply erased. They have to be resolved by using kindness and by reprogramming them through the use of Scripture (Ps. 119:9–11) and through being around others in the body of Christ.

To tell a person that he or she should not have certain feelings when they do exist is not being honest. Better to say, "I understand how you feel. Let's see what would be a godly approach to dealing with that feeling, and by all means let's be honest about it." It has been said that to be listened to is one of the most moving experiences in life. Also, we can remind ourselves of the saying that a burden shared is only half a burden. To allow a person to share true feelings is only common sense, and to understand is only kind.

Indeed, insight into one's personality (strengths, weaknesses, defenses) can help one to change for the better. Insight into how the past may be affecting the present is always in order. Insight into how past abuse, abandonment, and low self-image may be inappropriately applied today can be invaluable. Insight into unfair transference can be helpful. Insight can be helpful, but it is imperative that people move on in life and not remain in the past as depressed individuals are prone to do.

Help Them to Reprogram Their Thinking

We do not believe, as many behavioral therapists do, in the simple theory that a stimulus produces response. We believe that between the stimulus and response lies the individual's belief system. The importance lies not just in what happens to us in life; it is what we believe about what happens to us—our belief system. For example, the Christian should not view death as a non-Christian would.

Life is tough at times, but the Christian's belief system can change how he views life and can program his feelings and his physiological and behavioral response (2 Cor. 4:16–18). Romans 12:2 encourages us to be transformed by the renewing of our minds. Philippians 4:8 alerts us to being aware of our way of thinking. It is also easy for the Christian to personalize, magnify, and overgeneralize issues to focus on some minute detail without seeing the big picture. It is easy for us to make ourselves miserable by wanting everyone's love and approval, when God's love should be our satisfaction. It is easy for the Christian to feel that his unhappiness is externally caused and not to remind himself that Christ can make a huge difference. It is easy for the Christian to have beliefs that simply are not true (e.g., "God won't forgive me!" "God could never use me; I'm too weak!").

In some respects the mind can be compared to a huge computer, perhaps about the size of the Pentagon, with miles and miles of tapes. When new data are being evaluated, the mind scans through this vast library of tapes in search of knowing what kind of behavior, feeling, and physiological response to give. Our therapists claim the theory that the Christian can reprogram these tapes through the Word of God and through input by other Christians. Utilizing these tools can make a world of difference in the person's outlook on life. Consider the impact that the following verses could have on this concept: Deuteronomy 32:46–47; Joshua 1:8; Psalm 1:2–3; Isaiah 40:8; Jeremiah 5:14; Matthew 24:35; Luke 24:32; John 6:63; 15:7; 1 Thessalonians 2:13; 2 Timothy 3:16–17; Hebrews 11:3; and 1 John 2:14.

Use a Comprehensive and Balanced Approach Along with Common Sense

The approach should be comprehensive. What a sin to do therapy with someone for three years and then to realize you have been counseling a brain tumor. Medical disease should always be ruled out first. How a person feels is dependent on his medical condition. Man is one being—spirit, soul, and body. What affects one part invariably affects the other two. The medical, psychological, and spiritual should all be considered. Indeed, the approach should be comprehensive.

Second, the approach should be balanced. For example, to ignore the spiritual aspect is to forget what really counts in life—where one spends eternity. It is to forget that the secular schools have no standard of authority, such as the Bible. It is to forget that willpower can be ineffective (Rom. 7:18). It is to forget that man is basically selfish (Jer. 17:9). It is to forget that the Scriptures are not locked into any one specific approach—behavioral, cognitive, or insight oriented. The Scriptures are broad, and they are balanced.

To overemphasize the psychological is to forget that the non-Christian cannot understand the spiritual (1 Cor. 2:14). The other extreme is ignoring the psychological altogether and to doom some people to a life of psychosis and others to death. It is to ignore scientific knowledge in one field of medicine (psychiatry), while accepting it in other areas, such as internal medicine. It is to realize that many psychological problems have a medical aspect and to come across to a watching secular world as being ignorant and extreme.

To ignore the psychiatric problems is not to realize that a significant part of psychiatry is medical. I recall one missionary sent to us because she was "lazy." In reality, she had a brain tumor. I also recall a seminary student who came to us with a psychosis. His church pulled him out of treatment because they thought it was a spiritual problem. Of course, his behavior had spiritual and psychological dimensions; but there was also a base problem with the neurotransmitters within his brain. To ignore psychiatry altogether is not using common sense.

Third, a therapeutic approach should involve good common sense. I define this as knowing how to apply wisdom in day-to-day living. I recall one Christian counselor who became enthralled with one specific approach. He lost common sense when it came to helping people deal with feelings and became emotionally and physically involved with his clients, rationalizing in his mind that he was helping them. This is an extreme example of the loss of common sense, but there are many more subtle areas to which we could refer. We need to strive in Christian counseling to avoid extremes and to use common sense in all areas.

Remember the Importance of the Spiritual

Although man is comprehensive, the spiritual is the most important aspect of all. Eternity is forever. How could anyone overemphasize how important it is to know Christ and to spend eternity with him? To help someone solve his earthly problems and then ignore where he would spend eternity is useless. Individuals can be helped without knowing Christ, but he is a great power source in overcoming any spiritual or psychological problem. Although we do not understand it, we believe that Jesus Christ deeply enjoys spending time with us. To know him, enjoy him, to have a best friend in him is the most powerful resource on earth. Enoch must have felt some of this in Genesis 5:24, where we read that "Enoch walked with God" (KJV). Also, Moses must have felt some of this in Exodus 33:11, where it says, "And the LORD spake unto Moses face to face, as a man speaketh unto his friend" (KJV).

It is our prayer as Christian counselors that we may know Christ, walk with him, let him fill our inner beings; and then we will be able to help others because he is living in us.

See Resource J for further details.

Summary Questions for Chapter 6

Name seven steps of Christian counseling.	1. Be kind.
	2. Start with behavior.
	3. Help the counselee gain insight.
	4. Help with the resolution of feelings.
	5. Help the counselee reprogram his thinking.
	6. Use a comprehensive and balanced approach with common sense.
	7. Remember the importance of the spiritual.

7

Putting the Pieces Together: Why Christians Break Down and How the Christian Counselor Can Help

Why is life given to a man whose way is hidden, whom God has hedged in? For sighing comes to me instead of food; my groans pour out like water. What I feared has come upon me; what I dreaded has happened to me. I have no peace, no quietness; I have no rest, but only turmoil (Job 3:23–26 NIV).

The answer to why Christians have mental problems often relates to a complex interaction of spiritual, psychological, and physical factors. While it is true that spiritual issues may lie at the base of man's problems, in no way do they cancel out the psychological and physical factors.

Man, though a complex being, is one unit and should be treated accordingly. Understanding why Christians have mental problems requires dealing with man's different aspects—spiritual, physical, psychological—and showing the relationships between those parts and how they affect one another.

Man Is Spiritual

Man Is Lost

Basic to successful counseling and understanding man's nature is the realization that man without Christ is lost. Helping someone solve his present problem while ignoring his eternal destiny seems, at best, poor logic.

Man without Christ is lost (John 14:6) and eternally doomed to an eternal hell (Matt. 10:28; 2 Thess. 1:9). That belief has to affect the counseling process, "for the love of Christ controls us" (2 Cor. 5:14 NASB). The Christian counselor desires to see the counselee come to salvation through simply trusting Christ, believing he died for our sins (John 1:12; Rom. 3:23; 6:23). No single act has solved more problems and provided the potential for solving more conflicts, but each person must respond to Christ's finished work (John 6:37; Eph. 2:8–9).

Man Is Incomplete

Not only is man lost; he is incomplete. Unregenerate man faces an "existential" loneliness. He lacks the universe's deepest comfort and most powerful resource for solving problems—Jesus Christ.

Upon receiving Christ as Savior, a person finds that the Holy Spirit comes to indwell (1 Cor. 3:16), empower (Eph. 3:16), guide (Rom. 8:14), teach (John 14:26), and free him (Rom. 8:2).

He literally obtains God's resources, thus enabling him to live life fully (John 15:4, 7) and to cope with his problems (1 Pet. 5:7). The magnitude of a conflict's impact takes on a different perspective in a close walk with God (compare Moses in Exod. 33, Asaph in Ps. 73).

Man Is Physical

From the moment of birth, people say, man begins to die. After the age of forty, literally thousands of brain cells die daily.

Man constantly struggles against physical disease, but it can appear as a spiritual or psychological problem. Because man is a whole, his physical disease can lead to psychological or spiritual problems and vice versa.

Physical problems can produce emotional problems. For example, certain physical problems—viral illness such as mononucleosis or viral pneumonia, drug effects, cancer of the pancreas, multiple sclerosis—may produce symptoms of depression.

Certain physical problems can also produce psychotic symptoms or a loss of touch with reality. Among those physical problems are endocrine disorders, tumors of the brain's temporal lobe, effects of drugs, alcohol, and various medical diseases.

Furthermore, certain physical problems can produce symptoms of anxiety. These conditions include cardiovascular problems like mitral stenosis, endocrine disorders such as hyperthyroid and hypoglycemia, tumors, and effects from drugs. Some physical problems may even produce changes in personality. Perhaps the best known example is senility.

Emotional problems can produce physical problems. Stress, for instance, seems predisposed to illness in general. Doctors find that speed of recovery following infectious disease and surgical procedures correlate with a person's lifestyle and exposure to stress. A person's stress can also result in various psychophysiologic diseases such as ulcers, colitis, high blood pressure, etc.

Stress-oriented people who have a sense-of-time urgency are more prone to coronary artery disease. In addition and of utmost importance, stress can alter the nervous system's transmitters, thereby producing depression or psychosis.

Bereavement studies show that the deceased's first-degree relatives have a sevenfold increase in mortality rate the first year as compared to controls. Loneliness may be an important factor in developing coronary artery disease and susceptibility to some forms of cancer.

Emotional problems can appear as spiritual problems. Certain emotional or physical problems can appear spiritual in nature. A person with an impeding psychotic break may display an intense religious preoccupation. Someone having an obsessive-compulsive neurosis may struggle with a fear of having committed the unpardonable sin, or he may fear he hasn't really trusted Christ as Savior.

People diagnosed as having schizophrenia, obsessive-compulsive ego-alien thought, and multiple personalities are sometimes considered victims of demon possession. Demon voices, for example, would not respond to antipsychotic medication as do schizophrenics' "voices," which are merely auditory hallucinations.

Genetic factors. Finally, while we generally do not inherit psychological problems, we are physical and, therefore, inherit a certain physical (genetic) makeup that may make us more predisposed to certain psychological problems.

For example, schizophrenia occurs in only 1 percent of the general population. But if one parent is schizophrenic, then the risk goes up to 10 percent. If both parents are schizophrenic, it rises to 50 percent.

Studies with dizygotic twins (derived from two ova) yield interesting findings. If one becomes schizophrenic, there's a 10 percent risk the other will also. By contrast, in monozygotic twins (derived from one ova) the risk is around 50 percent, whether the twins are reared together or separated at birth.

In manic-depressive psychosis, relatives are affected twenty times more often than others in the general population. Twin studies (identical versus nonidentical) and adoption studies give near irrefutable data supporting that there is a genetic factor.

But perhaps the best proof in a manic-depressive psychosis comes from genetic linkage research. Studies show certain types of manic-depressive psychosis where the potential genetic weakness is actually carried (X chromosome).

In depression the family, twin, and adoption studies also point to the potential genetic weakness. For example, 30 percent of the depressives have a positive family history of depression.

If a nonidentical twin has depression, there's only a 10 percent chance the other will also have depression. If, however, the twins are identical, then the likelihood climbs to 76 percent. Even if they are reared separately, the chance of depression is around 67 percent.

I, personally, do not believe people generally inherit mental disorders. But I do believe the potential weakness is inherited, and this weakness can be manifested under stress and sinful choices.

In summarizing the physical aspect, the original premise is worth repeating. Man is a whole being. Physical disease can produce psychological symptoms, psychological stress can produce physical disease, and directly or indirectly spiritual issues lie at the core of both.

John Doe, a church elder, was referred by his pastor for professional help. A godly man, he had given years of dedicated service to the church. One day, however, he suddenly began to use obscene sexual language and make advances toward any women nearby. At the same time, he also increased his language about spiritual things. He seemed overtly involved in sin one minute while appearing superreligious the next.

Was the problem spiritual or psychological? Furthermore, was there any chance it could be physical? An evaluation revealed he had a specific type of seizure disorder with not only physical but also psychological and apparent spiritual manifestations. His seizure disorder was treated medically, and his functioning returned to normal.

Man Is Psychological

The word *psychology* is derived from the Greek word *psyche* (mind) and *logos* (word), meaning the study of the mind. The apostle Paul used the word *psychikas* (1 Cor. 2:14) to indicate the natural man. Although documentation seems unnecessary, we can, through Scripture, support the existence and function of the soul or self: mind (Ps. 139:14; Prov. 19:2), emotions (Song of Sol. 1:7), and will (Job 6:7; 7:15). The interrelationships between man's three realms demand that we understand the symptoms and causes behind psychological problems.

Symptoms are seldom seen in dramatic degrees outside formal psychological settings. Personality traits and various defense mechanisms, however, do exist to some degree in all of us. They are present in the Christian world, and knowledge of personality can affect the counseling process.

Psychological symptoms have causes. Psychological causes should in no way discount the spiritual aspect. Man is a whole. All aspects complement each other; they do not cancel one another out.

In examining causes, the counselor can consider early childhood without using it as an excuse. Brains are like computers, and the child's "computer" starts out essentially deprogrammed. By age six, however, it has obtained extensive programming. In fact, a computer the size of the Pentagon could not handle all the data a youngster's brain must process in decoding messages.

The brain's programming—and, therefore, its decoding and responding—can be significantly hindered if parents were absent, rejecting, possessive, harsh, seductive, cold, or overly submissive.

If the parents were absent, perhaps the child's dependency needs were not met. The individual is, therefore, more prone to depression or social maladjustments.

If parents do not allow the child to be an individual, he is more prone to schizophrenia. If they are harsh, the child may be driven by guilt, compulsiveness, a critical attitude, or paranoia. If parents are seductive or if they overly reward dramatic behavior, the child is more likely to have problems with hysteria. If both parents are in constant conflict, a child may be more prone to deep-seated insecurity and anxiety.

Man's unresolved conflicts often surface from childhood, and those struggles can intensify present-day problems. Man does have inner conflicts. Man is psychological. The key is not to use the psychological to excuse sin.

Putting the Pieces Together

Treatment of man's complex nature demands a comprehensive approach. Spiritual aspects are of utmost importance. Physical problems may be involved. Finally, psychological problems are often presiding and must be resolved.

In dealing with Elijah (1 Kings 19), God used a holistic approach—addressing each of man's three aspects. The Lord demonstrated how the spiritual, physical, and psychological realms are integrally related. They are bound to affect one another.

A competent counselor recognizes and deals with man's three aspects. His work will be governed by at least these four key principles:

First, a counselor's most basic concerns must center around the spiritual. Ministering to the spiritual aspect and producing a holy person can produce a healthy person.

Critical questions should include:

- Does the counselee know Christ?
- Does he need to examine passages such as Romans 3:23; 6:23; and John 1:12? In other words, does he need to hear the simple plan of salvation?
- Is the counselee spiritually immature and needing to grow in Christ? Would he benefit by the apostle Paul's advice, "Like newborn babes, long for the pure milk of the word, so that by it you may grow in respect to salvation" (1 Pet. 2:2 NASB).

Nothing, of course, can produce growth like nourishment from God's Word. In the Old Testament, God, through Moses, told the Israelites his word was their life (Deut. 32:46–47). He also said his word brings success (Josh. 1:8).

Blessed is the man who delights in God's Word (Ps. 1). He is like a fruitful tree, planted by the rivers of water. The psalmist compares rejoicing at God's Word to finding great spoil (119:162).

The Lord Jesus said, "Man shall not live by bread alone, but by every word that proceeds from the mouth of God" (Matt. 4:4 NKJV). He added that his words are spirit and life (John 6:63).

The apostles also placed special significance on God's Word. In Acts 20:32 Paul commended his hearers to God's Word for its ability to build them up. We note an apparent relationship between being strong and having God's Word abide in a person.

Because of man's nature, a counselor must be sensitive to using the Word when counseling. He himself needs to enjoy the Word, and that enjoyment must be evident to the counselee who may need help in knowing how to enjoy God's Word on a regular basis.

Sometimes a counselee is involved in a specific sin and needs help dealing with it. He may need gentle confrontation (Gal. 5:16). He may need support and encouragement from others within the body of Christ (Gal. 6:1) to prevent further hardening by the deceitfulness of sin. He will likely need protection from the sin by regularly spending time in God's Word (Ps. 119:8–11).

Second, a counselor must sensitively select an appropriate counseling approach. Among the many scriptural approaches we can apply in counseling are advice (Prov. 19:20), encouragement (2 Cor. 1:3–4), support (Rom. 1:11–12), education (the letters of the apostle Paul), corrective emotional experience (being a Christian example), support system (the body of

Christ), insight (parables of Christ), confession (James 5:16), positive verbal reinforcement (Rom. 1:8), modeling (Christ with the disciples), cognitive approach (Gal. 4:9), group work ("one another" passages), and confrontation (1 Thess. 5:14).

"To everything there is a season, a time for every purpose under heaven" (Eccles. 3:1, NKJV). There are times to be direct (Prov. 27:6), times to be indirect (2 Sam. 12:1–7). There are times to confront and times to encourage (1 Thess. 5:24). There are times to speak and times to listen (Eccles. 3:1, 7).

Sometimes Christ was matter-of-fact (Mark 10:14). At other times he was ever so gentle (Mark 10:16).

Some scriptural passages are appropriate for dealing with past sins (1 John 1:9) and others for focusing on the present (Matt. 6:34). Still others more appropriately point to the future (John 14:1–3). Some Scriptures focus on behavior (Gen. 4:6–7), others on feelings (e.g., the different emotions shown by Christ).

God's Word offers many approaches. This is only logical because not everyone has the same problem. Because of man's nature, his complexity, and the complexity of his problems, a counselor needs various approaches at his disposal.

Third, and even more important than the counseling approach, a counselor must model Christlikeness. Man's nature demands this because the counselee will identify with the counselor.

The counselor should be gentle and kind (2 Cor. 1:3–4; 10:1; Gal. 6:1; 1 Thess. 2:7, 11; 2 Tim. 2:24; Titus 3:2). Paul writes, "If I speak with the tongues of men and of angels, but do not have love, I have become a noisy gong or a clanging cymbal" (1 Cor. 13:1 NASB). Even scientific research verifies that successful counselors are those who demonstrate nonpossessive warmth, empathy, and genuineness. See Resource J at the back of this book for more details.

Finally, understanding the nature of man, a counselor must be sensitive to people who have physical or biochemical problems and will need professional referral. Toward potential suicidals, he needs to exercise sensitivity and be prepared to provide referral to a hospital. It is tragic to see cases where the family has refused because "professional help is not spiritual."

John Brown, a fifty-five year-old man, had received good care from several professionals (psychiatrist, pastor, etc.). But it seemed no one could manage to place his complexities into a unified whole. As a result, the man felt desperate. He was referred for medical investigation. The physicians discovered he had a biochemical problem that had been present for many years and was causing his depression. With medical treatments he found he could be more objective about the spiritual and psychological aspects.

Second, attention was given to the spiritual. Chaplains working on the case tried to model a kind, gentle, Christlike attitude. They also tried being more relaxed and having a carefree attitude around Mr. Brown, who had always seen God as strict, harsh, and "out to get him."

Finally, Mr. Brown began gaining psychological insight into some unresolved bitterness and fear. He experienced the pain of emotions. Fellow counselees gave him support and encouragement. He began implementing his insight and making appropriate behavioral changes. After one month of treatment, he felt better than he had felt in fifteen years.

The "whole man" needs attention. Man's blending of spiritual, physical, and psychological factors affect each part of the whole. To understand why Christians break down, or don't break down, we need to correlate and integrate the physical and psychological data with God-given spiritual principles.

Summary Questions for Chapter 7

1. Name a physical disease of an organ that can produce anxiety symptoms and another physical disease of the same organ that can produce depression.	Hyperthyroidism and hypothyroidism
2. True or False: Stress can cause physical disease in many different organs.	True
3. Name an emotional disease that appears spiritual at times and may start after an untreated streptococcal sore throat.	Obsessive-compulsive disorder

Applying the Christian Counseling Concepts: Examples of Biblical Homework Assignments to Be Given to the Counselee

Why homework assignments? Homework allows the counselee to put into practice vocalized beliefs. They also sensitize the counselee to spiritual, psychological, and physiological factors. The emphasis clearly needs to be on the spiritual. The following are merely examples. The Christian counselor may wish to learn from them as he makes up his own for the various problems in his counselees.

Homework Assignment 1
Beating Burnout

In the fall of 1900, a massive hurricane struck the Texas gulf coast. More than six thousand people lost their lives. Yet today, when hurricanes roar across the Atlantic to hit the east or south coasts, only a few lives are lost. Why? Because of advance warning systems, the danger signals can be heeded.

Just as meteorologists can now recognize certain signs as storm warnings of an approaching hurricane, so psychiatrists today can recognize the danger signals of approaching burnout that need to be heeded. By heeding these signals, irresponsible damage to the body and mind may be averted. How many of the following signals do you have?

Danger Signals	Yes	No
1. Exhaustion		
2. Detachment		
3. Cynical		
4. Irritable, inpatient		
5. Feeling unappreciated		
6. Change of attitude		
a. Withdrawal		
b. Increased dominance		
7. Paranoia		
8. Decreased concentration		
9. Increased health concerns		
10. Unfulfilled expectations		
11. Depression		
12. Suicidal thinking or just not wanting to live		

How did you do? How many of the twelve danger signals did you have? Is it time to reevaluate your situation? Are changes needed in your lifestyle? Are you in burnout?

Definition

Burnout is a state of mental, physical, or spiritual exhaustion. With the exhaustion comes a loss of enthusiasm, energy, idealism, perspective, and purpose. Too much personal or job stress over time results in burnout. Mentally the individual may feel disillusionment, failure, anger, cynicism, depression, guilt, apathy, decreased self-esteem, detachment, negativism, and a sense of helplessness. Physically the individual may have insomnia, weight changes, headaches, high blood pressure, and low energy. Spiritually the individual may have increasing questions and relate to Solomon: "So I hated life, because the work that is done under the sun was grievous to me. All of it is meaningless, a chasing after the wind" (Eccles. 2:17 NIV).

Burnout often starts with an external stressor (either job or personal) that leads to overextension that then leads to burnout and eventually to a clinical depression.

Voices Causing Burnout

Voices from childhood, colleagues, reality, or even chemicals all contribute to produce burnout. First, inner voices or drives from childhood that always demand more and more in production or performance may be behind a feeling of burnout. With this voice, whatever one accomplishes is not enough. Still, the voice pushes, "more, more, more." Second, colleagues may demand too much, not understanding that the Christian life starts with a yoke that is "easy" and is not driven by performance but by priorities (enjoying Christ and family). Third, reality at times (a financial problem, a difficult boss, and a demanding spouse) can be a voice producing burnout. Finally, with ongoing stress, brain chemicals can alter; and by so doing, they also become voices of burnout with feelings of guilt, gloom, and failure. In all of the above, the voices must be challenged and corrected. The voices are unfair, inappropriate, and inaccurate.

Treatments for Burnout

One of the most godly men who ever lived became burned out after mental and physical exhaustion (see Elijah in 1 Kings 19). God met Elijah's physical needs (sleep and food) initially.

- Do you need to meet your physical needs?
- Do you need a vacation, some sleep, some rest, good food? God also let Elijah ventilate even though his thinking was inaccurate. Do you need to share your burnout feelings?
- God then spoke to Elijah in a gentle, small voice. Do you need to let God encourage you with a great Scripture verse of hope?
- God also changed Elijah's task. Do you need to change your work situation?
- It has been said that insanity is doing the same thing over and over and expecting different results. Maybe your situation needs to change. Also, God sent Elijah a friend. Do you need a friend to stand beside you and help?
- In addition, God challenged Elijah's inaccurate thinking. Do you need to challenge your inaccurate thinking that is part of your burnout?
- How did you do? When will you take action to change your feelings of burnout?

Action to Overcome Burnout	Corrective Action	When to Start
1. Meeting physical needs		
a. sleep		
b. food		
c. vacation		
2. Sharing frustrations		
3. Memorizing Scripture verses for encouragement		
4. Changing pressure situations		
5. Finding a friend for support		
6. Challenging inaccurate thinking		
How many of the above six will you change?		

Medication Issues

New medications today make a major difference when burnout has gone too far and the chemistry of the brain has been altered by too much stress for too long. These medications can attack specific neurotransmitters and even subneurotransmitters of the brain, producing dramatic results.

The biochemistry of the brain is understood with great accuracy today. In many cases the chemistry can be shifted back to a normal state when burnout has clearly gone too far. The issue is not whether to medicate but effectiveness for Christ.

Homework Assignment 2
Fighting Worry

"Keep talking to him. Don't let him go to sleep," the old country doctor told the worried mother as her fifteen-year-old son lay near death with diabetes mellitus. I was that son in the early sixties. I had good reason to have a realistic concern, but if left unchecked, that concern would have turned to worry that surely would have killed me. Through Christ I learned ten precious lessons on how to deal with worry.

For these lessons to be effective, you may want to apply one of these steps daily for the next three months as you learn them personally ("If you teach a man anything, he will never learn," Bernard Shaw).

Develop a Driving Desire to Overcome Worry

It is not easily abated, but it is a must ("Those who do not learn to fight worry die young," Alexis Carrel). Worry is no doubt a factor in many medical diseases such as heart disease, high blood pressure, some cancers, and even physiological and neurological changes of depression and anxiety ("The Lord may forgive us our sins, but the nervous system never does," William Lowry). We lost only about one-third of a million men during World War II, compared to about one-half a million per year to heart disease, much of which is worry related. ("The greatest mistake physicians make is that they attempt to cure the body without attempting to cure the mind; yet the mind and the body are one and should not be treated separately," Plato). The Bible states the concept even better in 1 Thessalonians 5:24.

I recall one of my first psychiatric patients years ago. She told me she was a chronic worrier. She appeared to be forty-five years old; she was only thirty-five years old. The years of worry had taken their toll. Not only does worry age us; it also may be related to infections; worry tends to decrease the lymphocytes, which fight off disease. Also, cancer patients who worry intensely do not seem to do as well. Furthermore, worry triggers the autonomic nervous system, which can be a factor in disease of many organs. In one research study, six of ten heart patients had constricted coronary arteries and decreased blood flow to their heart following emotionally triggered events and worry. Also, if a first-degree relative dies, then one's chance of dying at any point in time within the next year is increased sevenfold. Worry truly kills. Many years ago in New York City, there were a few outbreaks of smallpox. "A few might die," shouts of warning ran throughout the city. How much more should we shout the warning today and offer methods of inoculation?

Contemplation question: On a scale of zero to ten, how strong is your desire to overcome worry?

Decipher the Odds

Probably 95 percent of the issues we worry about never come true. You might want to make a list of your top five worries five years ago, ten years ago, and twenty years ago. What percent came true? Do you even recall what the worries were?

Contemplation question: What are the odds of your current worries coming true?

See the Big Picture

Many times we worry over issues that are really minor issues when we consider the big picture. The big picture may be life or death—a life to live for Christ. You might imagine that you have only one week to live. Now, are all those worries worth it?

Contemplation question: In the light of eternity, are most of your worries major or minor?

Live One Day at a Time

Two thousand years ago the best advice I know was given for worry: "Take therefore no thought for the morrow: for the morrow shall take thought for the things of itself. Sufficient unto the day is the evil thereof" (Matt. 6:34 KJV). I have often reminded myself to work at living one day at a time. "No man knows the future," I tell myself. "I must enjoy Christ and focus on today." Worriers tend to live in the future, to live for a tomorrow that never comes. Obsessive individuals tend to live in worry of the future, and depressive individuals tend to live in worry of the past. No man knows what tomorrow may bring, and no man can change the past. God holds tomorrow, and he forgives the past. The future is not here, and the past is gone forever. We can only live in the present.

Contemplation question: What percent of your worries are about the past that is gone forever or the future that is not yet here?

Get the Facts

I have found that many issues I want to worry about fade when I get more facts. Perhaps I have made false assumptions or unlikely predictions. Perhaps my initial interpretation was inaccurate. Perhaps the facts are not as bad as my subjective emotional reading on a subject.

Contemplation question: What facts can you gather today that will help you fight your worries?

Form a Plan of Action

When I want to worry, I sit down and formulate a plan of action to attack the problem. I write down the problems and many options for attack. I then pick a few good options and start to implement the plans. The taking of action gets my mind off the worries and starts actions that may make a difference. Einstein said that a man is what he repeatedly does. Why not do what is healthy instead of just worry?

Contemplation question: What is a specific godly plan for attacking your worries?

Share with a Friend

It has been said that a burden shared is only half a burden. This is one of the most powerful techniques I know. I would recommend building a few good friendships and sharing with those friends any worries on a daily basis. "Two are better than one; because they have a good reward for their labour. For if they fall, the one will lift up his fellow: but woe to him that is alone when he falleth; for he hath not another to help him up" (Eccles. 4:9–10 KJV). "A friend is a present you give yourself" (Robert Louis Stevenson). Of course, the best friend we can ever have is

Christ. He loves for us to share our worries with him. He wants us to become less worry oriented and more heaven oriented, where the days of worries will no longer exist.

Contemplation question: With whom do you share, and who holds you accountable not to worry?

Realize God Is Still in Control

Sometimes I laugh at myself. I hear myself say, "Well, there is nothing else I can do; I guess I will just have to pray." Pray to the God of the universe; pray to the one who can do anything; pray to someone who is omniscient, omnipresent, and omnipotent; pray to someone who can erase a problem in one thousandth of a second. Then I ponder and laugh. "Cast all your anxiety on him because he cares for you" (1 Pet. 5:7 NIV). "Until now you have not asked for anything in my name. Ask and you will receive, and your joy will be complete" (John 16:24 NIV). I remind myself that God has never lost control. He can take care of any of my troubles.

Contemplation question: How much do you believe God is really in control?

Face the Inevitable and if Not the Inevitable, Accept the Possible

I used to worry over having diabetes. Then I decided that diabetes, for me, was a reality and that worrying over having it would not change it. What I could do was to take action to prevent possible medical side effects of the disease. I turned from worry to action, and that action worked. I have had diabetes for forty years, and I am still healthy and without side effects. In fact, diabetes was a major tool God used in helping me develop discipline that helped me to have a ministry for Christ. Sometimes issues are not inevitable but are more of a possibility. In those cases it may help to prepare to accept the worst and improve on it. Perhaps good can come from the apparent bad. "And we know that all things work together for good to them that love God, to them who are the called according to his purpose" (Rom. 8:28 KJV).

Contemplation question: In your life, what is the inevitable? Have you accepted it?

Choose Against Worry

There is a choice involved in worry. Let's choose against it for ourselves and for the cause of Christ. "Wherefore seeing we also are compassed about with so great a cloud of witnesses, let us lay aside every weight, and the sin which doth so easily beset us, and let us run with patience the race that is set before us, looking unto Jesus the author and finisher of our faith; who for the joy that was set before him endured the cross, despising the shame, and is set down at the right hand of the throne of God. For consider him that endured such contradiction of sinners against himself, lest ye be wearied and faint in your minds" (Heb. 12:1–3 KJV).

Contemplation question: Would you choose against worry today?

Homework Assignment 3
Guilt and Freedom: Nine Actions One Can Take

As a youth, I avoided the "great" sins. Yet, of the more negative-oriented emotions (anger, anxiety, depression, fear, shame, and guilt), guilt was the one that bothered me the most as a youth. It was an uncomfortable and a somewhat tormenting-type feeling. Perhaps you still feel that way today. Here are nine suggestions that I pray may help. It may be time to lighten up and move on for Christ.

Accept Christ and His Forgiveness

This concept may seem basic, but it is the foundational starting point for overcoming guilt. We have all committed sin. We are all guilty. Christ died in payment for our sins. When we accept this, we are forgiven—no universal guilt should exist.

Many Christians know the above experientially but at times may not feel it. So just in case you might need encouragement again—you are forgiven.

In Psalm 103:12–14 the following words of comfort are recorded: "As far as the east is from the west, so far hath he removed our transgressions from us. Like as a father pitieth his children, so the LORD pitieth them that fear him. For he knoweth our frame; he remembereth that we are dust" (KJV). In regard to the above verses, Jennings states, "God remembers what man forgets (our infirmities); man remembers what God forgets (our sins)" (Dake, 1961, p. 596).

Claim 1 John 1:9 When Needed

Sometimes even dear saints need to be reminded that 1 John 1:9 is still in the Bible and always will be. It states, "If we confess our sins, he is faithful and just to forgive us our sins, and to cleanse us from all unrighteousness" (KJV). When we sin and break fellowship with God, a simple confession can restore fellowship immediately. The confession may not remove all of the consequences of sin, but it can be a major help in abating guilt for wrongs committed.

Ask Yourself if the Guilt Has Gone Too Far

I believe that guilt can go too far, that it can be inappropriate. In 1 John 3:20 the following is recorded: "For if our heart condemn us, God is greater than our heart, and knoweth all things" (KJV). Individuals with obsessive worry issues will clearly carry guilt too far. In some cases this can have a physiological dimension (serotonin and neurotransmitter depletion). Years later, obsessive and depressive Christians may not let go of some wrong committed months or years before, even when the wrong is very minor and long since confessed and forgiven by Christ. At times there may be a physiological component and medication (SSRIs—Selective Serotonin Reuptake Inhibitors) may make a major difference.

Ask if the Guilt Has Not Gone Far Enough

This point is unlikely to apply to those who would read such an article as this, but it should be included for completeness. First John 3:8–9 states: "The one who practices sin is of the devil; for the devil has sinned from the beginning. The Son of God appeared for this purpose, to destroy the works of the devil. No one who is born of God practices sin, because His seed abides in him; and he cannot sin, because he is born of God" (NASB). Charles Ryrie, in regard to the above verse, states in the *The Ryrie Study Bible:* "Practices = continually practices, i.e., sins as a regular way of life . . . Habitual actions indicate one's character. Seed. I.e., the divine nature given the one born of God . . . This nature prevents the Christian from habitually sinning" (Ryrie, 1978, p. 1882).

Challenge Inappropriate Thinking

Thinking is inappropriate when a person keeps having guilty thoughts such as "I can never be forgiven"; "there is no corrective action I can take now"; "I am the most horrible person in the world"; "this is the end of the world." This kind of thinking needs to be challenged, and a more realistic belief should be offered immediately: "God can forgive me"; "I can attempt corrective action as much as possible and reasonable"; "God can help me deal with this"; "God still loves me"; "I can and will change with God's help." Even very godly people (King David) have sinned and later dealt with it.

Share Your Guilty Feelings

Find an appropriate person (God, parent, pastor, friend, mate, counselor, lawyer) and share the guilty feeling. Do not carry the feelings alone. The organs of the body were never built to withstand the stress of guilt. Psalm 32:3–5 declares: "When I kept silent about my sin, my body wasted away through my groaning all day long. For day and night Thy hand was heavy upon me; my vitality was drained away as with the fever heat of summer. I acknowledged my sin to Thee, and my iniquity I did not hide; I said, 'I will confess my transgressions to the Lord'; and Thou didst forgive the guilt of my sin" (NASB).

Take Appropriate Actions of Reconciliation

Two very helpful verses appear in Matthew 5:23–24. "Therefore if you are presenting your offering at the altar, and there remember that your brother has something against you, leave your offering there before the altar and go; first be reconciled to your brother, and then come and present your offering" (NASB).

Avoid Future Sin and Resulting Guilt

Satan is a genius. He entices people to swap moments of pleasure for days, months, and years of guilt. Let's refuse Satan's deceptive implorement. Proverbs 4:15 states: "Avoid it, pass not by it, turn from it, and pass away" (KJV).

Utilize Behavior Techniques

Feelings of any kind (guilt included) are difficult to deal with directly since feelings tend to some degree to have a mind of their own. They are not easily abated at will. However, they will often give way to a focus on behavior. If the guilt in your mind will not abate, then get up and do something. Get out of the mind trap and focus on healthy behavior. Stay busy.

Conclusion

As one of God's children was reading an encyclopedia, he exclaimed, "Praise the Lord!"

One asked, "What is there in an encyclopedia to elicit praise to God?"

"Sir, I just read that the ocean is five miles deep in some places!"

"But how does that call for praise to God?"

"Have you never read," asked the praiseful Christian, "of God's promise to all who seek His mercy and forgiveness: 'Thou wilt cast all their sins into the depths of the sea' (Mic. 7:19)?"

Oceanographers tell us that there are depths of the sea which have lain motionless for eons and that no surface storms, however violent, dredge up the forgiven and forgotten sins of God's children when they are submerged in the depths of God's love and forgetfulness: "Their sins and their iniquities will I remember no more" (Heb. 8:12) (Knight, 1984, p. 114–15).

Many of you are very godly people—perhaps among the most godly alive today—and yet you have wrestled with guilt. You have no doubt learned some valuable lessons. What would you add? You have done all of the above. Is it time to lighten up and move on for Christ?

Homework Assignment 4
Knowing the Will of God:
Eight Questions to Discerning God's Will

Many sincere Christians ask me, "Is what I am about to do the will of God?" What an excellent but often difficult question to answer. Perhaps part of the problem is the lack of a clear set of questions that could be used to answer the question. Below are eight questions I hope you will find beneficial in knowing God's will for an issue you are facing. The questions range from very definitive to more difficulty to ascertain with certainty. Even the very definitive questions may be too general in scope for a person's particular question. Thus, the question of God's will is a good one but sometimes a difficult one. With this in mind you may also want to look for a pattern.

For example, if several of the eight questions are no or questionable, then be cautious. If all eight are yes, then the likelihood of being in God's will increases greatly. I wish you the best on your quest for knowing God's will in a particular area of your life. Perhaps George W. Truett stated the importance of the principle best when he said, "To know the will of God is the greatest knowledge. To do the will of God is the greatest experience" (Knight, 1984, p. 320).

The first eight letters of the alphabet (A, B, C, D, E, F, G, H) help you remember each question. Incidentally, some of the eight questions have several subquestions to help you reach an answer for that specific question.

Asking God's Help in Knowing His Will Was Done

God desires to let us know his will. "If any of you lack wisdom, let him ask of God, that giveth to all men liberally, and upbraideth not; and it shall be given him. But let him ask in faith, nothing wavering. For he that wavereth is like a wave of the sea driven with the wind and tossed" (James 1:5–6 KJV). "I will instruct thee and teach thee in the way which thou shalt go: I will guide thee with mine eye" (Ps. 32:8 KJV).

Contemplation question: Have you asked God what his will is?

Behavior, Attitude, and Character Inventory Measure Up

As I studied the issue of knowing God's will, it seemed that a foundation principle had to do with behavior, attitude, and character-type issues. These were sort of prerequisite issues. However, as these are examined, we need to realize that no one is perfect, and again, a pattern is very helpful if it exists. Here are the subquestions for reaching an overall answer.

- Are you doing God's will in a broader context?

	Yes	No
1. Are you obedient to God's revealed will in the Bible in obvious areas?		
2. Are you seeking God's interests first?		
3. Will this help you directly or indirectly to lead others to Christ?		
4. Are you depending on God to enable you to do His will? "For it is God which worketh in you both to will and to do of his good pleasure" (Phil. 2:13 KJV).		
5. Do you enjoy doing God's will, and is God's Word in your heart? "I delight to do thy will, O my God: yea, thy law is within my heart" (Ps. 40:8 KJV).		
6. Are you living a good, godly life? "For so is the will of God, that with well doing ye may put to silence the ignorance of foolish men" (1 Pet. 2:15 KJV).		
7. Are you growing in Christ and avoiding overt sin such as lust? "For this is the will of God, even your sanctification, that ye should abstain from fornication" (1 Thess. 4:3 KJV).		
8. Are you giving thanks "in everything?" "In every thing give thanks: for this is the will of God in Christ Jesus concerning you" (1 Thess. 5:18, KJV).		
9. Are you overly focused on some specific detail in regard to the will of God, and perhaps somewhat oblivious to extremely important principles concerning the will of God, such as spending time with Christ, taking care of your family, etc.?		

- Will this particular action help you . . .

	Yes	No
1. Not hurt others?		
2. Glorify God?		
3. Not be enslaved to some issue?		
4. Grow in Christ?		
5. Be holy "in your conversation"?		
6. Be involved in discipling others for Christ?		

Contemplation question: Overall, do the various questions relating to behavior, attitude, and character give a yes answer to your decision?

Circumstances Vote Yes

Circumstances relating to a decision should be considered. "But I would ye should understand, brethren, that the things which happened unto me have fallen out rather unto the furtherance of the gospel; so that my bonds in Christ are manifest in all the palace, and in all other places; and many of the brethren in the Lord, waxing confident by my bonds, are much more bold to speak the word without fear" (Phil. 1:12–14 KJV).

Contemplation question: Do circumstances vote yes for your decision?

Defying Logic Is Not an Issue

We do need to think carefully through the logic of a proposed plan of action. God's will may very well be consistent with our logic. Would your choice defy logic for God's purpose for your family responsibilities or for other obvious reasons? However, here again there may be dangers since God's will can be above our apparent logic; so just a word of caution.

Contemplation question: Is your proposed action logical? Does it make sense in general and overall logic? Is defying logic not an issue?

"Experts" Agree on the Proposed Plan of Action

There certainly can be wisdom in counselors. "Without counsel purposes are disappointed: but in the multitude of consellors they are established" (Prov. 15:22 KJV).

Here again caution should be given. No other person may know for sure God's will for you in some matters. Helpful questions might be:

	Yes	No
1. Were several counselors asked for input?		
2. Are the counselors Christlike?		
3. Do they fully understand the scope of the decision?		

Contemplation question: Do "experts" or godly counselors agree that this is probably God's will for you?

Feelings Vote Yes

What people sense in the feelings of their spirit is very important. The problem here may be a misunderstanding in where the feelings are originating. Are they originating from personality issues, from carnal elements, or from God's Spirit? I have seen Christians confuse the various dimensions. Also, some Christians are so strict in their conscience that they have no feelings of peace about any decision, and others have peace in a decision even when it clearly goes against God's revealed and very obvious truth in the Bible. Having feelings of peace ("And let the peace of God rule in your hearts, to the which also ye are called in one body; and be ye thankful," Col. 3:15 KJV) can be important. They are not always present since God's will may be against our will (Jonah).

Contemplation question: Do your feelings give you peace about this decision?

God's Word Votes Yes

God is never inconsistent with his revealed will in the Bible. If a course of action goes against his revealed will, then it simply is not his will. God's Word speaks on many specific issues. What does the Bible say about your area of question? Be careful about going against it. However, the Bible at times may not speak directly to a specific decision. Then, a good question might be, Is this decision consistent with principles in God's Word?

Contemplation question: Is this decision in agreement with God's revealed will in the Bible?

Health Issues Do Not Significantly Interfere in the Decision-Making Process

Health issues can blur the decision-making process at times. Individuals with more obsessive and paranoid personality traits may be too rigid in making a decision. Individuals with more sociopathic, hysterical, and borderline traits may not be rigid enough. Also, clarity of thinking is important. This could be blurred in any kind of organic brain process—Alzheimer's, multi-infarct dementia, head injury, etc. Also, psychiatric issues such as depression can blur objectivity, and psychoses can alter interpretation. Finally, almost any kind of medical, psychological, or spiritual issues can blur judgment at times.

Contemplation question: Are you relatively free of any medical, psychological, or spiritual issue that might significantly blur your judgment and decision-making process?

Conclusion

	Yes	No
1. Have you asked God what his will is?		
2. Overall, do the various questions relating to behavior, attitude, and character give a yes answer to your decision?		
3. Do circumstances vote yes for your decision?		
4. Is your proposed action logical? Does it make sense in general and overall logic? Is defying logic not an issue?		
5. Do "experts" or godly counselors agree that this is probably God's will for you?		
6. Do your feelings give you peace about this decision?		
7. Is this decision in agreement with God's revealed will in the Bible?		
8. Are you relatively free of any medial, psychological, or spiritual issue that might significantly blur your judgment and decision-making process?		

How did you do? How many yes answers did you obtain from the eight areas of reference in regard to knowing God's will?

Congratulations on being serious enough to want to know God's will in a specific area in your life. My prayers are with you. May God grant your wish for wisdom.

Homework Assignment 5
Losing Weight

1. Would you be willing to memorize and ask God to help you apply 1 Corinthians 6:19–20 to your life?
   - "Or do you not know that your body is the temple of the Holy Spirit who *is* in you, whom you have from God, and you are not your own? For you were bought at a price; therefore glorify God in your body and in your spirit, which are God's" (1 Cor. 6:19–20 NKJV).
2. Do you have a problem with food?
   - Do you eat for comfort?
   - Is your eating out of control at times?
   - Are you embarrassed by your weight?
3. Do you have an unhealthy reason for overeating?
   - To avoid intimacy?
   - To cope with stress?
   - To cope with unresolved issues in your past?
4. Would you make specific choices to succeed?
   - Be gentle with yourself. Accept yourself as you are but improve as necessary for the cause of Christ.
   - Identify food as an addiction.
   - Pray to God daily about your problem.
   - Ask a friend to hold you accountable. Claim James 5:16: "Confess your trespasses to one another, and pray for one another, that you may be healed. The effective, fervent prayer of a righteous man avails much" (NKJV).
   - Do weight control for the right motive—to be more effective for Christ.
   - Eat a well-balanced diet but less of it. Avoid simple sugars and high fat foods.
   - Stop using food for recreation.
   - Stop using food for stress relief.
   - Count calories in your diet.
   - Avoid junk food.
   - Exercise in moderation at home and as appropriate.
   - Keep a journal of your progress.
   - Forgive yourself quickly for any relapse by claiming 1 John 1:9: "If we confess our sins, He is faithful and just to forgive us our sins and to cleanse us from all unrighteousness" (NKJV).
   - Develop new interests. Some of these should center around your local church.

Homework Assignment 6
Overcoming Poor Grades—How to Make A's
Twelve Days to Twelve Tools

Are you having trouble with poor grades at school, and is this affecting you emotionally? Do you want to make A's? Well, certain tools may make a major difference. In going through the equivalent of about twenty-six years of school (grade school, junior high school, high school, college, medical school, rotating internships, psychiatry residency, board certification, seminary, and Ph.D. work), these are the techniques I used. I suggest you study and apply one technique per day for twelve days.

Day 1: Do It for the Right Goals

Let's face it. Good grades are big business. They may very well determine what university you attend, what graduate school you attend, what job you obtain, and what your financial future holds.

However, there is a much greater goal. Why not do it for Jesus Christ? This goal may enable you to endure and actually make those A's. Good grades may allow you to enter a field of study that will give you a platform for a ministry for Christ. I strove to make A's so I could go to medical school, and I wanted to go to medical school because I saw a ministry for Christ in it. Nothing but a major goal would have been enough. "And whatsoever ye do, do it heartily, as to the Lord, and not unto men" (Col. 3:23 KJV).

Contemplation question: Is your goal strong enough to enable you to make A's?

Day 2: Believe You Can Do It

Do you believe you can make A's? Many students can make A's if they know how and believe they can.

Both Albert Einstein and Thomas Edison made D's at one time. Theodore Roosevelt said, "The average man who is successful is not a genius. He is a man who has merely ordinary qualities to a more than ordinary degree." Henry Ford said, "If you think you can do well in school, you're right. If you don't think you can do well in school, you're still right."

Abraham Lincoln could have been destroyed by being average (poor, ungainly appearance, etc.), but instead he went on to greatness. He once said, "God must have loved the common man because He made so many of them." Average people become successful not because of their IQs but because of qualities such as self-discipline, social skills, keeping promises, bouncing back from death, and having another who brought out the best in them. Are you average? That's not a problem; but you must believe you can do it. You must believe you can be successful in the classroom. "And Moses said unto God, Who am I, that I should go unto Pharaoh, and that I should bring forth the children of Israel out of Egypt? And he said, Certainly I will be with thee; and this shall be a token unto thee, that I have sent thee" (Exod. 3:11–12a KJV).

Contemplation question: Given the right tools, do you believe you can make A's?

Day 3: Attend Class and Take Good Notes

This may sound easy and it is, so why not do it? Students who make good grades attend class, often sit on the front row, and take good notes. In medical school I would summarize each page of notes, and on the back of that page I would list the top three points. I would then very quickly review these notes daily. I always figured that teachers would ask what they discussed, and I was right.

Contemplation question: Except for extreme and unavoidable reasons, are you willing to attend class and take good notes every time?

Day 4: Use Your Time Wisely

Using time wisely was one of the best tools I had. I would always carry small summary cards of my notes and would quickly review them when I had spare moments during the day or night. Those and other *spare moments* made all the difference.

Another point in regard to the use of time is that I have always been inclined to attack large study and work projects in *bite-size* parts. I literally have used spare moments to write about fifty books, and the use of spare moments allowed me to make many A's.

In regard to time use, I also worked in agreement with my *biological clock.* I am more alert at night, so I studied more at night. Also in regard to time use, the well-worn advice of having an *organized place to study* is well given—comfortable, books, equipment, and good lighting.

Finally, *computers* are a must for time management. Computers are allowing people to do in moments what took hours in wasted time.

Contemplation question: Would you be willing to make a commitment today to find creative ways to use "spare moments" on a daily basis to improve your grades?

Day 5: Know Your Instructor

Knowing an instructor may start before you ever enroll in a class. If you have a choice and know an instructor has some cause that is out of balance (never gives A's, is unusually harsh or rigid, etc.), then be careful about signing up for that class. Let that teacher prove his cause somewhere else.

Once you are in the class, let the teacher know of your interest in the class and your desire to do well. Ask for his or her suggestions for learning the information. Ask if extra points are routinely allowed for extra projects. In short, get to know the teacher.

Contemplation question: Would you be willing to set up a special meeting with each of your teachers?

Day 6: Learn Test-Taking Skills

Test-taking skills helped me in grades from grade school to relatively recent years. In medicine a person is licensed by the state. A few years ago I decided I wanted to be licensed in a state that required a very broad general medical background, a background that I had been taught in previous years. I passed the test. I had studied, but I also had excellent test-taking skills. Here are some principles used.

- If permitted, use different but similar tests that were either used in the past or prepared for study.
- Know the type of test questions (essay or objective specifics), and prepare accordingly.
- In objective-type tests, "all of the above" is more likely to be a better choice than "none of the above."
- In true-false questions, "all," "never," and "always" questions are often false.
- When general terms are used ("most," "some," "usually," and "might"), true is usually the better answer.
- In multiple choice questions where two of four answers are opposites, then one of the opposites may be a good choice.
- Answer every question as you go with your best guess. Your initial impression may be the best.
- Read the directions carefully.
- Get to the test site early and stay late.
- Keep track of time.
- Write neatly in essay questions.
- Because of short-term memory, do cram (but be reasonable).
- Have a positive attitude. Attitude can make a big difference.

Contemplation question: How many of the above thirteen points can you now repeat by memory?

Day 7: Utilize Special Helps

We are blessed today with many special helps that are available to many people—tutors, special classes in public school, special schools from grade school through college (for example, the University of Arizona has a special division for individuals with ADHD—Attention-Deficit/Hyperactivity Disorders), schools that specialize in a low students-to-teacher ratio.

You may be like I was and essentially too poor to afford special helps or tutors. God can still help. I recall when God sent a young pastor to our church who was simply brilliant and volunteered to teach me geometry, which to some degree launched my pursuit of math and science. God's hands are not tied. Be creative; look and check around for special helps.

Contemplation question: Should you seek special help? If so, which one will you seek?

Day 8: Improve Your Memory

A good memory is partially inherited, but techniques may take an average memory and make it superb. Dario Donatelli, who broke the world record for digital memory, said, "My memory is like anyone else's. There are probably hundreds of thousands of other people who, if they had the same interest in numbers and saw a reason to practice calculating and memory for years, would be faster than I am."

High school and college require lots of memory work. To some degree, studying means memorizing. To some degree, memorizing is the heart and core of learning. Here are the techniques to practice:

Desire. Almost every schoolteacher will tell you that desire is a real key to good school performance and memory. In fact, a good memory will have ramifications far beyond the production of A's in school. Theodore Roosevelt's campaign manager never forgot a name, and this may be one reason for Roosevelt's success. Good grades and memory must start with a desire.

Observation. You cannot remember what you never learned. Would you work on your observation skills in regard to people, names, and events?

Association and other memory techniques. This is often a key component to good memory.

George Bidder was born in England in 1806. He was known as a child prodigy in calculations. As a youth he developed such questions as: "If a flea springs two feet, three inches every hop, how many hops must it take to go around the world with the circumference being twenty-five thousand miles?" Later in his life when in the House of Lords, one colleague said that Mr. Bidder should not be allowed to remain in the room because nature had endowed him with qualities that did not place his opponents on a fair testing. However, when asked how he did it, his explanation clearly revealed it was not all genetics. He clearly used mnemonic techniques.

It is often helpful to associate new information with old information. For example, in learning the treble clef in music (E, G, B, D, F), one might recall the old saying of "Every Good Boy Does Fine." In geography, Italy is easily remembered by many because it is shaped like a boot.

In addition to associations, rely upon the ridiculous, upon *exaggerations* (for example, to remember a person by the name of Longman, visualize that he is very long or tall—exaggerate it in your mind) and upon *links* (for example, to remember a grocery list, work on linking one item to the next in some manner).

Also, *acronyms* may help. For example, in medical school I learned the symptoms of dementia with "IMAJO" (meaning impairment in Intellect, Memory, Affect, Judgment, and Orientation).

Many good books can help you increase your memory skills such as *The Memory Book* by Jerry Lucas and Harry Lorayne. Others include *Don't Forget* by Danielle C. Lapp, *Brain Builders* by Richard Leviton, and *Super Memory Super Student: How to Raise Your Grades in 30 Days* by Harry Lorayne.

Contemplation question: On a scale from one to ten (one being poor and ten being excellent) would you be willing to compare how you do now and one month from now?		
	Now	Later
A. Desire		
B. Observation skills		
C. Association skills		
D. Exaggeration method		
E. Links method		
F. Acronym method		

Day 9: Improve Your Reading Skills

In junior high school I developed reading skills that have served me well. If I had one hour to read an assignment, I would adhere to the following schedule:

- Preview, two minutes. I would quickly preview the chapter titles, the subtitles, and any paragraph titles of the entire chapter.
- Scan, eight minutes. I would very rapidly read the entire chapter.
- Break, two minutes. I would take a quick break and perhaps do ten pushups or just walk around. A brief affirmation always helped.
- Read, thirty-five minutes. I would read the material more slowly this time.
- Break, five minutes. I would take a little longer break to relax in order to be able to concentrate better.
- Study, ten minutes. I would make a brief outline and try to commit what I could to memory; in short, I would study.
- Total time allowed for reading, one hour. One hour spent in reading. There are many courses today that improve reading skill and help in rapid reading:
  Hooked on Phonics: (800) 346-5455
  Action Reading: A fast-track phonics reading program. (800) 378-1046 or (623) 465-0195.

Contemplation question: Are the above suggestions enough to help you, or should you in addition take a special reading course?

Day 10: Improve Your Vocabulary

Words are the tools of thought. Success is often linked to vocabulary. Every creative idea in the universe began with words. For years, I have enjoyed reading vocabulary books. I found that words are fun. It is very helpful to find a book or system that you enjoy. Helpful books include:

- *Rapid Vocabulary Builder,* Norman Lewis, MacFadden-Bartell Book
- *It Pays to Increase Your Word Power,* Peter Funk, A Bantam Book
- *Word Power Made Easy,* Norman Lewis, Pocket Books
- *Vocabulary Program* (videotape), Bergen Evans, Success Motivation Cassettes
- *Power Vocabulary,* Elizabeth Morse-Cluley and Richard Read, Webster's NewWorld
- *Up Your S.A.T. Score,* Larry Berger, Manek Mistry, and Paul Rossi, New Chapter Press
- *Verbal Workbook for the SAT,* Walter James Miller, Gabriel P. Freedman, Elizabeth Morse-Cluley, and Margaret A. Haller, Prentice Hall Press
- *1100 Words You Need to Know,* Murray Bromberg and Melvin Gordon, Barron's Educational Series, Inc.
- *504 Absolutely Essential Words,* Murray Bromberg, Julius Liebb, and Arthur Traiger, Barron's Educational Series, Inc.
- *30 Days to a More Powerful Vocabulary*
- *The Children's Visual Dictionary*
- *Curious Kids Go to Preschool: Another Big Book of Words*
- *Basic Phrasal (NTC English-Language References)*

- *Arthur's Really Helpful Word Book*
- Hundreds of vocabulary boosters and tutors are available through the Internet on www.amazon.com or 800-201-7575.

Contemplation question: Would you be willing to learn one new word per week?

Day 11: Treat Any Medical or Emotional Issue

I have seen countless children and adolescents over the years whose grades progress from C's to A's by medically treating their ADHD (Attention-Deficit/Hyperactivity Disorder). I have seen others whose grades improve significantly and their acting-out behavior and anger abate by treating their depression or anxiety. I have seen others improve their grades by getting their diabetes under better control. When their hemoglobin A/C (a reflection of their diabetic control) goes down, their grades often go up.

A missing key for some is the treatment and management of any medical or emotional condition.

Contemplation question: Do you have any medical or emotional condition that needs medical treatment and management?

Day 12: Understand How People Learn Differently and Accentuate Your Learning Style

People learn differently. Some are more auditory (10 percent perhaps); others are more visual (20 percent perhaps); and others are more tactile. Some people learn better in groups; others learn better alone. Some people learn better moving around as they study; others by being stationary.

Some people are more left brained (deliberate, in control of feelings, past or future oriented, remember details), while others are more right brained (spontaneous, free with feelings, present oriented, senses more, and see the whole picture better than the details). Most teachers are probably more left brained. I would suggest that you capitalize on where you are strong and help develop more where you are lacking. Successful people (like Einstein) seemed to have both.

Contemplation question: Are you emphasizing courses according to your gifts? Do you have any specific way to develop the area that might be lacking? Do you try to relate to others in the manner that might be strong in them, visual versus auditory versus tactile, or right brain versus left brain? Remember people relate best based on their innate aptitudes.

Conclusion

Do you want to make A's? The tools above may hold the key. After two weeks (implementing one tool per day), how did you do? After two months, how did you do? After two years, how did you do?

Evaluation

		Two weeks	Two months	Two years
Day 1	Did you have strong goals?			
Day 2	Did you believe you could make A's?			
Day 3	Did you attend class and take good notes?			
Day 4	Did you use your time wisely?			
Day 5	Did you get to know each instructor?			
Day 6	Did you learn specific test-taking skills?			
Day 7	Did you avail yourself of special helps?			
Day 8	Did you learn new memory techniques?			
Day 9	Did you improve your reading skills?			
Day 10	Did you take specific steps to improve your vocabulary?			
Day 11	Did you seek any needed medical or emotional helps?			
Day 12	Do you use your natural learning style and work on areas where you may be lacking in innate ability?			
Grade Point Overall				

Progress

How did you do? If you did well, then congratulations. If you did not do well, then just start over. Ask Christ to help you. Best wishes.

Homework Assignment 7
Ten Techniques for Handling Anger Appropriately

I grew up in a rough, tough John Wayne mentality of a community. Anger was often handled, inappropriately, by just physically fighting. I recall as a youth when the pastor was taken out behind the church and received a beating for preaching too directly. (If ministers today think they have it rough, well, it may have been worse then.) Today we are equally bad, perhaps. We often give great psychological tools without the emphasis on Christ. With these psychological tools, people can become adept at psychologically beating up one another. Let's pray that with a Christlike sensitivity we can handle anger appropriately. Much may be at stake for the cause of Christ.

Realize the Importance of Handling Anger Appropriately

First, the medical importance of handling anger appropriately is immense. In fact, the single factor most likely to cause a heart attack in the American adult is not high cholesterol, smoking, or a history of heart disease in the family; rather, the greatest danger is chronic exposure to hostile interactions with other people. Furthermore, death rates are four to seven times higher in people who are hostile, cynical, and suspicious than in people who are not as angry.

Angry, cynical people are five times as likely to die under age fifty as people who are calm and trusting. Also, the question has been raised whether there is a cancer-prone personality—passive, suppressing of anger, and withdrawn. Finally, depression (with possible anger) is a better predictor of heart attacks than existing artery damage, high cholesterol, or cigarette smoking. Anger is probably the number-one health risk in America and probably the leading cause of death.

Second, anger with unforgiveness and resulting bitterness not only hurts one spiritually but can also hurt many others: "Looking diligently lest any man fail of the grace of God; lest any root of bitterness springing up trouble you, and thereby many be defiled" (Heb. 12:15, KJV).

Third, though never proven, anger has long been postulated as a major factor in many psychological depressions.

Contemplation question: Has anger possibly been a factor in any of your health issues?

Gain Insight into Unresolved Anger

Gain insight into unresolved anger of the past that affects the present and gain insight into possible anger in the personality. It is very difficult to deal with a problem if you do not recognize it. If you find yourself overreacting to a person today, it may be because of transference from anger in the past. Of course, this is not fair to the current recipient of the anger and will not resolve the damaged emotions of the past. Many disorders today may have anger evident to others but partially hidden to the individual (major depressive disorder with repressed anger; post-traumatic stress disorder with much fear and anger remaining; personality disorders with maladaptive behavior patterns involving anger such as the borderline personality with possible abandonment issues; the paranoid with possible physical-abuse issues; the hysteric with possible sexual-abuse issues; the obsessive-compulsive with possible verbal-abuse issues; or adjustment disorders originating from conflict with much resulting anger). Insight into any of the above may be a great first step.

Contemplation question: Is there significant unresolved anger in your past that might be affecting you today? Do others see anger in you that you don't see?

Share the Anger

Sharing the anger can be like a burden lifted. It has been said that a burden shared is only half a burden. The sharing could be with a wise friend, a counselor, and most of all, with God.

Contemplation question: Do you have anyone you share your anger with on a daily or weekly basis?

Express the Anger

Anger can be turned inward, possibly resulting in depression and bitterness; it can be turned outward in an aggressive manner, provoking anger and hurt in others; or it can be dealt with in a gently assertive, Christlike manner. Ephesians 4:15 may be a good verse to apply here: "But speaking the truth in love, may grow up into him in all things, which is the head, even Christ" (KJV).

Contemplation question: In the last month, what percent of the time, when expressing anger, were you passive versus aggressive versus assertive?

Sublimate the Anger

Sublimation is a defense mechanism whereby a person takes hostile energy and expresses it in an acceptable manner (exercise, housework, etc.) initially in order to get it under control. For example, a person may be so angry that if he tried to express it he would be aggressive, so sublimation is used first.

Contemplation question: When was the last time you used a sublimation technique? What was your technique?

Use Helpful Behavioral Techniques

Many techniques may help with anger resolution. For example, writing a letter to the offending party and then tearing it up may help; writing a letter but framed in a positive manner may help; etc. One behavior technique that many of us learned as children might be a good one to try again—count to ten before responding.

Contemplation question: Should you write a letter?

Use Spiritual Helps

Forgive and turn the issue over to God. Forgiveness starts with the will, not the emotions. Emotional resolutions of feelings take time, so forgiveness must start with a simple choice of the will. Interestingly enough, this act of the will releases God to act on our behalf. "Dearly beloved, avenge not yourselves, but rather give place unto wrath: for it is written, Vengeance is mine; I will repay, saith the Lord" (Rom. 12:19 KJV).

There are often five major parties that may have offended us: parents, mate, self, others, and even God. Of course God has done nothing wrong, but in our ignorance we may not understand why he allowed something to happen to us.

Contemplation question: Who are the top three people who have offended you? Have you, with your will, forgiven them and asked God to deal with them in his wisdom?

Ask God for divine help. God obviously does not want us to remain angry and unforgiving. "Forbearing one another, and forgiving one another, if any man have a quarrel against any: even as Christ forgave you, so also do ye" (Col. 3:13 KJV). Also, "Let all bitterness, and wrath, and anger, and clamour, and evil speaking, be put away from you, with all malice; and be ye kind one to another, tenderhearted, forgiving one another, even as God for Christ's sake hath forgiven you" (Eph. 4:31–32 KJV). And yet anger may be so difficult that we repeatedly need to ask God for help as we claim his promises. "There hath no temptation taken you but such as is common to man: but God is faithful, who will not suffer you to be tempted above that ye are able; but will with the temptation also make a way to escape, that ye may be able to bear it" (1 Cor. 10:13 KJV).

Contemplation question: When was the last time you shared with God that this one (anger) has you by the throat and you need his help?

Grow in Christ. Growing in Christ may really help. "But the fruit of the Spirit is love, joy, peace, longsuffering, gentleness, goodness, faith, meekness, temperance" (Gal. 5:22–23 KJV). Much of my anger is not righteous indignation but rather results from my being somewhat selfish or suspicious. Whatever the cause, growing in Christ can help.

Contemplation question: Because of your growth in Christ, does your anger flare less often now than in the past?

Make a choice against letting the anger escalate. A few years ago as I was reading the Book of Proverbs, I noticed that there is a choice involved in anger. "He that is slow to wrath is of great understanding" (Prov. 14:29a KJV).

Contemplation question: Have you ever started to become angry and with each thought your anger escalated?

Consider Medication

In some cases medication can make a major difference. For example, in depression with anger, a group of medications known as the Selective Serotonin Reuptake Inhibitors (SSRIs— Prozac, Paxil, and Zoloft) may make dramatic difference. There has been talk of working toward approval of these drugs in more severe Premenstrual Syndrome (PMS) with its associated depression and anger. Also, many other drugs have been suggested as possibly helping in various conditions with anger and aggression: beta blockers such as Inderal and Visken; mood stabilizers such as Lithium, Depakote, Tegretol, and perhaps Neurontin; minor tranquilizers such as Ativan and BuSpar; dopamine agents such as Risperdal, Seroquel, and Zoloft; and Attention Deficit/Hyperactivity Disorder agents such as Adderall.

Contemplation question: Are your depression and anger to the degree that medication could help? Should you talk with a medical doctor or psychiatrist?

Use Reality Therapy and Cognitive Therapy on Yourself

Ask yourself if there is an appropriate action that you can take that would help. Ask yourself if you need to challenge your thinking. Are you overly personalizing, magnifying, or generalizing? Are you focusing too much on a few negatives and ignoring many positives? Are you assuming things that may not be true? Are you reasoning more from emotions than actual facts? We all do the above, and we all need to challenge thinking that increases anger unduly.

Contemplation question: When was the last time that you needed to challenge your thinking because you were personalizing, magnifying, generalizing, or using emotional reasoning?

Deal with Anger Quickly

Anger should be dealt with quickly. "Be ye angry, and sin not: let not the sun go down upon your wrath" (Eph. 4:26 KJV).

Contemplation question: Anger can cause great damage spiritually, emotionally, and medically. Do you deal with your anger as much as possible the day it happens?

Conclusion

Anger can be handled in appropriate ways. I have listed ten of the best ways. Which three would work best for you? Which three would give you the most trouble? Consider working on one of the above daily for a week and then picking another one. Rate your anger on a scale from one to ten (ten being high intensity). Rate yourself now and then again in two and one-half months.

Summary Questions for Chapter 8	
1. The following defines what? "A quick reference guide similar to Cliff Notes but designed for the Christian counse-lee to help him or her deal with the problems in a pragmatic fashion."	Christian Homework Assignments
2. What do homework assignments accomplish?	They allow the counselee to put into practice vocalized beliefs
3. True or False: It is reasonable that if secular behavioral tools can change brain chemistry for the better as docu-mented by PET scans of the brain, God's Word could do much more.	True

Resources for Christian Counselors

The Christian counselor is often in need of specific information on a variety of topics—quick reference material that is summarized. The following documents include important phone numbers, examples of mental evaluations, a list of psychiatric medications, an overview of secular schools of psychotherapy, DSM-IV diagnostic codes, a list of physical diseases that produce emotional problems, a list of the medical effects of stress on the body, genetic factors in psychological problems, characteristics of mental disorders, and skills needed by a Christian counselor.

Statement of Beliefs and Mission for a Christian Counseling Facility

Our purpose is to meet the needs of the body of Christ through helping believers deal with their issues so they can be more effective workers for the kingdom of Christ.

The main avenue to accomplish the purpose and mission of this ministry is to make available appropriate, Christ-centered counseling or mentoring.

Our Beliefs

We believe that there is one true God, who exists in three persons: the Father, the Son, and the Holy Spirit.

We believe that Jesus Christ is God's Son. He was born of a virgin as both fully God and fully man, lived a sinless life, died in our place as a sacrifice for the sins of mankind, was buried, arose bodily from the grave, ascended into heaven, and will literally return to earth.

We believe that the Holy Spirit is the divine helper, assistant, counselor, and instructor; and his work is to reveal Christ, convict of sin, lead to repentance, guide believers, comfort, strengthen, and sanctify the soul.

We believe that the Bible is the inspired Word of God, without any error, and is the sole authority for life and faith.

We believe human beings are the special creations of God, made in his image. They fell through the sin of the first man, Adam, and all human beings are sinners in need of salvation.

We believe salvation is by grace through faith in Jesus Christ as one's Savior. Every person who is saved is eternally secure in the Lord Jesus Christ and will spend eternity in heaven, while those who die without Christ will spend eternity in hell forever separated from God.

We believe each believer has direct access to God through the Lord Jesus Christ.

We believe the church is a local body of baptized believers with the Lord Jesus Christ as the head. And we believe in the importance of the church for worship, service, missions, encouragement, and growth of its members.

We believe that all issues should be thoroughly evaluated through the grid of Scripture and that Scripture always holds the final authority.

RESOURCE B

Billing and Insurance

Billing and insurance systems vary widely from all-cash systems with single receipts and deposits to a complete department dedicated to insurance, collections, posting, and billing to outside agencies that handle all of the billing aspects. Since these systems vary so widely and are outside the scope of this book, other than a mention, no attempt is made here to deal with these systems.

Some systems are nonprofit and based on donations. Other systems are for profit only and are based on fee for service. And still other systems are nonprofit but charge a fee.

Characteristics of Mental Disorders

1. Psychoses
   a. *Schizophrenia* is a severe mental disorder characterized by the "four A's" (flat [nonexpressive] affect, loose associations, ambivalence, and autism), bizarre behavior, hallucinations, and/or delusions.
   b. *Brief reactive psychosis* follows a stressful event and lasts less than two weeks.
   c. *Atypical psychosis* is also short-lived but unlike brief reactive psychosis cannot be traced to any known cause of stress.
   d. *Schizoaffective disorder* is marked by both schizophrenic and affective symptoms.
2. Anxiety Disorders
   a. *Generalized anxiety disorder* is characterized by free-floating tension and worry.
   b. *Phobia* is irrational fear.
   c. *Obsessive-compulsive disorder* involves anxieties which develop after a traumatic event.
   d. *Somatoform disorder (Briquet's syndrome)* involves multiple somatic complaints that are secondary to anxiety.
   e. *Psychogenic-pain disorder* is marked by complaints of pain without a physical cause.
   f. *Hypochondriasis* is an obsessive fear that one has a serious disease.
3. Personality Disorders
   a. *Paranoid personalities* are suspicious and hypersensitive, and project their own faults onto others.
   b. *Obsessive-compulsive personalities* desire to control themselves and others, and they fall into the traps of workaholism and perfectionism.
   c. *Hysterical personalities* are emotional, excitable, and exhibitionistic.

    d.   *Passive-aggressive personalities* are prone to procrastination, forgetfulness, and stubbornness.

    e.   *Passive-dependent personalities* have such a low degree of self-confidence that they allow others to assume responsibility.

    f.   *Sociopathic personalities* have a problem of self-identity, demonstrating instability in their moods and friendships.

    g.   *Narcissistic personalities* have a long-standing, grandiose preoccupation with self.

    h.   *Schizoid personalities* are characterized by aloofness.

    i.   *Avoidant personalities* desire but shun social relationships because of a hypersensitivity to rejection.

    j.   *Schizotypal personalities* occasionally manifest very eccentric, almost psychotic behavior.

    k.   *Cyclothymic personalities* are characterized by alternating moods (from high to low).

    l.   *Dysthymic personalities* display a depressed mood.

4. Substance Abuse

The abuse of drugs results in physical addiction and social complications.

5. Organic Mental Disorders

    a.   *Dementia* is a progressively severe brain disorder characterized by disorientation and impairment of intellectual functions.

    b.   *Delirium* is a state of clouded consciousness.

    c.   *Organic amnestic syndrome* involves loss of memory.

    d.   *Organic delusional syndrome* involves an irrational clinging to false beliefs.

    e.   *Organic hallucinosis* causes a person to see or hear things that are not really there.

    f.   *Organic affective syndrome* is characterized by depression.

    g.   *Organic personality syndrome* involves a distinct change from one's usual temperament.

6. Affective Disorders

    a.   *Manic-depressive disorder* is marked by mood swings reaching psychotic levels.

    b.   *Major depression* involves extreme symptoms (both psychological and physical) of depression.

7. Adjustment Disorder

Maladaptive reactions (anxiety, depression, or withdrawal) to a specific stress often result in affective disorders.

8. Disorders Appearing in Early Life (Infancy, Childhood, or Adolescence)

    a.   *Mental retardation* is subaverage intellectual functioning.

    b.   *Attention-deficit disorder* is an inability to concentrate for more than a very limited period of time.

    c.   *Conduct disorder* involves repeated patterns of antisocial behavior.

    d.   *Anxiety disorder* is characterized by unwarranted tension and worry.

    e.   *Identity disorder* is distress over a number of those elements by which one establishes himself as an individual (lifetime goals, career, friends, sex, sense of morality, religion, etc.).

f. *Anorexia nervosa* is characterized by a drastic weight loss due to an intense fear of becoming fat.
g. *Bulimia* is binge eating followed by forced vomiting.
h. *Motor-tic disorder* involves recurrent, involuntary, purposeless movements, particularly of the eye or face.
i. *Tourette's disorder* involves motor tics and multiple vocal tics.
j. *Stuttering* is a spasmodic hesitation in speaking, or a repetition or prolongation of sounds or words.
k. *Enuresis* is an involuntary voiding of urine.
l. *Encopresis* is a voluntary or involuntary passing of feces at inappropriate times.
m. *Infantile autism* is a gross and sustained impairment in social relationships which appears before the age of thirty months.
n. *Specific developmental disorder* is a delay in the rate of learning a particular skill such as language, reading, or arithmetic.
o. *Reactive attachment disorder* is characterized by poor emotional and physical development.
p. *Elective mutism* is refusal to speak.
q. *Oppositional disorder* is active or passive resistance to authority figures.
9. Impulse-Control Disorders
    a. *Pathological gambling* is repeated engagement in betting to the point of social disruption.
    b. *Kleptomania* is an obsessive impulse to steal.
    c. *Pyromania* is an uncontrollable impulse to set fires.
    d. *Explosive disorder* involves repeated outbursts of aggression.
10. Sexual Disorders
    a. *Transsexualism* is an overwhelming desire to be the opposite sex.
    b. *Paraphilia* is sexual arousal in abnormal ways (fetishism, transvestism, zoophilia, pedophilia, exhibitionism, voyeurism, sadism, masochism).
    c. *Psychosexual dysfunction* covers a wide spectrum of problems, including inhibited sexual desire, frigidity, impotence, difficulties with orgasm, premature ejaculation, painful intercourse, and vaginismus.

RESOURCE D

DSM-IV Classification of Mental Disorders

This is the official classification of mental disorders used worldwide. The Christian counselor is often called upon to recognize this terminology.

Disorders Usually First Diagnosed in Infancy, Childhood, or Adolescence

Mental Retardation

Note: These are coded on Axis II (see Multiaxial System at end of this resource).

317	Mild Mental Retardation
318.0	Moderate Mental Retardation
318.1	Severe Mental Retardation
318.2	Profound Mental Retardation
319	Mental Retardation, Severity Unspecified

Learning Disorders

315.00	Reading Disorder
315.1	Mathematics Disorder
315.2	Disorder of Written Expression
315.9	Learning Disorder NOS

Motor Skills Disorder

315.4	Developmental Coordination Disorder

Communication Disorders

315.31	Expressive Language Disorder
315.31	Mixed Receptive Expressive Language Disorder
315.39	Phonological Disorder
307.0	Stuttering
307.9	Communication Disorder NOS

Pervasive Developmental Disorders

299.0	Autistic Disorder
299.80	Rett's Disorder
299.10	Childhood Disintegrative Disorder
299.80	Asperger's Disorder
299.80	Pervasive Developmental Disorder NOS

Attention-Deficit and Disruptive Behavior Disorders

314.xx	Attention-Deficit/Hyperactivity Disorder
314.01	Combined Type
314.00	Predominantly Inattentive Type
314.01	Predominantly Hyperactive-Impulsive Type
314.9	Attention-Deficit/Hyperactivity Disorder NOS
312.8	Conduct Disorder
	Specify type: Childhood-Onset Type/Adolescent-Onset Type
313.81	Oppositional Defiant Disorder
312.9	Disruptive Behavioral Disorder NOS

Feeding and Eating Disorders of Infancy or Early Childhood

307.52	Pica
307.53	Rumination Disorder
307.59	Feeding Disorder of Infancy or Early Childhood

Tic Disorders

307.23	Tourette's Disorder
307.22	Chronic Motor or Vocal Tic Disorder
307.21	Transient Tic Disorder
	Specify if: Single Episode/Recurrent
307.20	Tic Disorder NOS

Elimination Disorders

___.___	Encopresis
787.6	With Constipation and Overflow Incontinence
307.7	Without Constipation and Overflow Incontinence
307.6	Enuresis (Not Due to a General Medical Condition)
	Specify type: Nocturnal Only/Diurnal Only/Nocturnal and Diurnal

Other Disorders of Infancy, Childhood, or Adolescence

309.21	Separation Anxiety Disorder
	Specify if: Early Onset
313.23	Selective Mutism
313.89	Reactive Attachment Disorder of Infancy or Early Childhood
	Specify type: Inhibited Type/Disinhibited Type
307.3	Stereotypic Movement Disorder
	Specify if: With Self-Injurious Behavior
313.9	Disorder of Infancy, Childhood, or Adolescence NOS

Delirium, Dementia, and Amnestic and Other Cognitive Disorders

Delirium

293.0	Delirium due to . . . [*Indicate the general medical condition*]
___.___	Substance Intoxication Delirium (*refer to Substance-Related Disorders for substance-specific codes*)
___.___	Substance Withdrawal Delirium (*refer to Substance-Related Disorders for substance-specific codes*)
___.___	Delirium Due to Multiple Etiologies (*code each of the specific etiologies*)
780.09	Delirium NOS

Dementia

290.xx	Dementia of the Alzheimer's Type, With Early Onset (*also code 331.0 Alzheimer's Disease on Axis III*)
290.10	Uncomplicated
290.11	With Delirium
290.12	With Delusions
290.13	With Depressed Mood
	Specify if: With Behavioral Disturbance
290.xx	Dementia of the Alzheimer's Type, With Late Onset (*also code 331.0 Alzheimer's Disease on Axis III*)
290.0	Uncomplicated
290.3	With Delirium

290.20	With Delusions
290.21	With Depressed Mood
	Specify if: With Behavioral Disturbance
290.xx	Vascular Dementia
290.40	Uncomplicated
290.41	With Delirium
290.42	With Delusions
290.43	With Depressed Mood
	Specify if: With Behavioral Disturbance
294.9	Dementia Due to HIV Disease *(also code 043.1 HIV infection affecting central nervous system on Axis III)*
294.1	Dementia Due to Parkinson's Disease *(also code 332.0 Parkinson's Disease on Axis III)*
294.1	Dementia Due to Huntington's Disease *(also code 333.4 Huntington's Disease on Axis III)*
290.10	Dementia Due to Pick's Disease *(also code 331.1 Pick's Disease on Axis III)*
290.10	Dementia Due to Creutzfeldt-Jakob Disease *(also code 046.1 Creutzfeldt-Jakob Disease on Axis III)*
___.___	Substance-Induced Persisting Dementia *(refer to Substance-Related Disorders for substance-specific codes)*
___.___	Dementia Due to Multiple Etiologies *(code each of the specific etiologies)*
294.8	Dementia NOS

Amnestic Disorders

294.0	Amnestic Disorder Due to . . . [*Indicate the general medical condition*]
	Specify if: Transient/Chronic
___.___	Substance-Induced Persisting Amnestic Disorder *(refer to Substance-Related Disorders for substance-specific codes)*
294.8	Amnestic Disorder NOS

Other Cognitive Disorders

294.9	Cognitive Disorder NOS

Mental Disorders Due to a General Medical Condition Not Elsewhere Classified

293.89	Catatonic Disorder Due to . . . [*Indicate the general medical condition*]
310.1	Personality Change Due to . . . [*Indicate the general medical condition*]
	Specify type: Labile Type/Disinhibited Type/Aggressive Type/Apathetic Type/Paranoid Type/Other Type/Combined Type/Unspecified Type
293.9	Mental Disorder NOS Due to . . . [*Indicate the general medical condition*]

Substance-Related Disorders

[a] *The following specifiers may be applied to Substance Dependence:*
With Physiological Dependence/Without Physiological Dependence
Early Full Remission/Early Partial Remission
Sustained Full Remission/Sustained Partial Remission
On Agonist Therapy/In a Controlled Environment
The following specifiers apply to Substance-Induced Disorders as noted:
[I]With Onset During Intoxication/[W]With Onset During Withdrawal

Alcohol-Related Disorders

Alcohol Use Disorders

303.90	Alcohol Dependence[a]
305.00	Alcohol Abuse

Alcohol-Induced Disorders

303.00	Alcohol Intoxication
291.8	Alcohol Withdrawal
	Specify if: With Perceptual Disturbances
291.0	Alcohol Intoxication Delirium
291.0	Alcohol Withdrawal Delirium
291.2	Alcohol-Induced Persisting Dementia
291.1	Alcohol-Induced Persisting Amnestic Disorder
291.x	Alcohol-Induced Psychotic Disorder
.5	With Delusions[I,W]
.3	With Hallucinations[I,W]
291.8	Alcohol-Induced Mood Disorder[I,W]
291.8	Alcohol-Induced Anxiety Disorder[I,W]
291.8	Alcohol-Induced Sexual Dysfunction[I]
291.8	Alcohol-Induced Sleep Disorder[I,W]
291.9	Alcohol-Related Disorder NOS

Amphetamine (or Amphetamine-Like)-Related Disorders

Amphetamine Use Disorders

304.40	Amphetamine Dependence[a]
305.70	Amphetamine Abuse

Amphetamine-Induced Disorders

292.89	Amphetamine Intoxication
	Specify if: With Perceptual Disturbances

292.0	Amphetamine Withdrawal
292.81	Amphetamine Intoxication Delirium
292.xx	Amphetamine-Induced Psychotic Disorder
.11	With Delusions[I]
.12	With Hallucinations[I]
292.84	Amphetamine-Induced Mood Disorder[I,W]
292.89	Amphetamine-Induced Anxiety Disorder[I]
292.89	Amphetamine-Induced Sexual Dysfunction[I]
292.89	Amphetamine-Induced Sleep Disorder[I,W]
292.9	Amphetamine-Related Disorder NOS

Caffeine-Related Disorders

Caffeine-Induced Disorders

305.90	Caffeine Intoxication
292.89	Caffeine-Induced Anxiety Disorder[I]
292.89	Caffeine-Induced Sleep Disorder[I]
292.9	Caffeine-Related Disorder NOS

Cannabis-Related Disorders

Cannabis Use Disorders

304.30	Cannabis Dependence[a]
305.20	Cannabis Abuse

Cannabis-Induced Disorders

292.89	Cannabis Intoxication
	Specify if: With Perceptual Disturbances
292.81	Cannabis Intoxication Delirium
292.xx	Cannabis-Induced Psychotic Disorder
.11	With Delusions[I]
.12	With Hallucinations[I]
292.89	Cannabis-Induced Anxiety Disorder[I]
292.9	Cannabis-Related Disorder NOS

Cocaine-Related Disorders

Cocaine Use Disorders

304.20	Cocaine Dependence[a]
305.60	Cocaine Abuse

Cocaine-Induced Disorders

292.89	Cocaine Intoxication
	Specify if: With Perceptual Disturbances
292.0	Cocaine Withdrawal
292.81	Cocaine Intoxication Delirium
292.xx	Cocaine-Induced Psychotic Disorder
.11	With Delusions[I]
.12	With Hallucinations[I]
292.84	Cocaine-Induced Mood Disorder[I,W]
292.89	Cocaine-Induced Anxiety Disorder[I,W]
292.89	Cocaine-Induced Sexual Dysfunction[I]
292.89	Cocaine-Induced Sleep Disorder[I,W]
292.9	Cocaine-Related Disorder NOS

Hallucinogen-Related Disorders

Hallucinogen Use Disorders

304.50	Hallucinogen Dependence[a]
305.30	Hallucinogen Abuse

Hallucinogen-Induced Disorders

292.89	Hallucinogen Intoxication
292.89	Hallucinogen Persisting Perception Disorder (Flashbacks)
292.81	Hallucinogen Intoxication
292.xx	Hallucinogen-Induced Psychotic Disorder
.11	With Delusions[I]
.12	With Hallucinations[I]
292.84	Hallucinogen-Induced Mood Disorder[I]
292.89	Hallucinogen-Induced Anxiety Disorder[I]
292.9	Hallucinogen-Related Disorder NOS

Inhalant-Related Disorders

Inhalant Use Disorders

304.60	Inhalant Dependence[a]
305.90	Inhalant Abuse

Inhalant-Induced Disorders

292.89	Inhalant Intoxication
292.81	Inhalant Intoxication Delirium
292.82	Inhalant-Induced Persisting Dementia

292.xx	Inhalant-Induced Psychotic Disorder
.11	With Delusions[I]
.12	With Hallucinations[I]
292.84	Inhalant-Induced Mood Disorder[I]
292.89	Inhalant-Induced Anxiety Disorder[I]
292.9	Inhalant-Related Disorder NOS

Nicotine-Related Disorders

Nicotine Use Disorder

305.10	Nicotine Dependence[a]

Nicotine-Induced Disorders

292.0	Nicotine Withdrawal
292.9	Nicotine-Related Disorder NOS

Opioid-Related Disorders

Opioid Use Disorders

304.00	Opioid Dependence[a]
305.50	Opioid Abuse

Opioid-Induced Disorders

292.89	Opioid Intoxication
	Specify if: With Perceptual Disturbances
292.0	Opioid Withdrawal
292.81	Opioid Intoxication Delirium
292.xx	Opioid-Induced Psychotic Disorder
.11	With Delusions[I]
.12	With Hallucinations[I]
292.84	Opioid-Induced Mood Disorder[I]
292.89	Opioid-Induced Sexual Dysfunction[I]
292.89	Opioid-Induced Sleep Disorder[I,W]
292.9	Opioid-Related Disorder NOS

Phencyclidine (or Phencyclidine-Like)-Related Disorders

Phencyclidine Use Disorders

304.90	Phencyclidine Dependence[a]
305.90	Phencyclidine Abuse

Phencyclidine-Induced Disorders

292.89	Phencyclidine Intoxication
	Specify if: With Perceptual Disturbances
292.81	Phencyclidine Intoxication Delirium
292.xx	Phencyclidine-Induced Psychotic Disorder
.11	With Delusions[I]
.12	With Hallucinations[I]
292.84	Phencyclidine-Induced Mood Disorder[I]
292.89	Phencyclidine-Induced Anxiety Disorder[I]
292.9	Phencyclidine-Related Disorder NOS

Sedative-, Hypnotic-, or Anxiolytic-Related Disorders

Sedative, Hypnotic, or Anxiolytic Use Disorders

304.10	Sedative, Hypnotic, or Anxiolytic Dependence[a]
305.40	Sedative, Hypnotic, or Anxiolytic Abuse

Sedative-, Hypnotic-, or Anxiolytic-Induced Disorders

292.89	Sedative, Hypnotic, or Anxiolytic Intoxication
292.0	Sedative, Hypnotic, or Anxiolytic Withdrawal
	Specify if: With Perceptual Disturbances
292.81	Sedative, Hypnotic, or Anxiolytic Intoxication Delirium
292.81	Sedative, Hypnotic, or Anxiolytic Withdrawal Delirium
292.82	Sedative-, Hypnotic-, or Anxiolytic-Induced Persisting Amnestic Dementia
292.83	Sedative-, Hypnotic-, or Anxiolytic-Induced Persisting Amnestic Disorder
292.xx	Sedative-, Hypnotic-, or Anxiolytic-Induced Psychotic Disorder
.11	With Delusions[I,W]
.12	With Hallucinations[I,W]
292.84	Sedative-, Hypnotic-, or Anxiolytic-Induced Mood Disorder[I,W]
292.89	Sedative-, Hypnotic-, or Anxiolytic-Induced Anxiety Disorder[W]
292.89	Sedative-, Hypnotic-, or Anxiolytic-Induced Sexual Dysfunction[I]
292.89	Sedative-, Hypnotic-, or Anxiolytic-Induced Sleep Disorder[I,W]
292.9	Sedative-, Hypnotic-, or Anxiolytic-Related Disorder NOS

Polysubstance-Related Disorder

304.80	Polysubstance Dependence[a]

Other (or Unknown) Substance-Related Disorders

Other (or Unknown) Substance Use Disorders

304.90	Other (or Unknown) Substance Dependence[a]
305.90	Other (or Unknown) Substance Abuse

Other (or Unknown) Substance-Induced Disorders

292.89	Other (or Unknown) Substance Intoxication
	Specify if: With Perceptual Disturbances
292.0	Other (or Unknown) Substance Withdrawal
	Specify if: With Perceptual Disturbances
292.81	Other (or Unknown) Substance-Induced Delirium
292.82	Other (or Unknown) Substance-Induced Persisting Dementia
292.83	Other (or Unknown) Substance-Induced Persisting Amnestic Disorder
292.xx	Other (or Unknown) Substance-Induced Psychotic Disorder
.11	With Delusions[I,W]
.12	With Hallucinations[I,W]
292.84	Other (or Unknown) Substance-Induced Mood Disorder[I,W]
292.89	Other (or Unknown) Substance-Induced Anxiety Disorder[I,W]
292.89	Other (or Unknown) Substance-Induced Sexual Dysfunction[I]
292.89	Other (or Unknown) Substance-Induced Sleep Disorder[I,W]
292.9	Other (or Unknown) Substance-Related Disorder NOS

Schizophrenia and Other Psychotic Disorders

Schizophrenia

295.xx	Schizophrenia
	The following Classification of Longitudinal Course applies to all subtypes of Schizophrenia.
	Episodic with Interepisode Residual Symptoms (*Specify if:* With Prominent Negative Symptoms/Episodic with No Interepisode Residual Symptoms)
	Continuous (*Specify if:* With Prominent Negative Symptoms)
	Single Episode in Partial Remission (*Specify if:* With Prominent Negative Symptoms/Single Episode in Full Remission)
	Other or Unspecified Pattern
.30	Paranoid Type
.10	Disorganized Type
.20	Catatonic Type
.90	Undifferential Type
.60	Residual Type
295.40	Schizophrenia Disorder
	Specify if: Without Good Prognostic Features/With Good Prognostic Features
295.70	Schizoaffective Disorder
	Specify type: Bipolar Type/Depressive Type
297.1	Delusional Disorder
	Specify type: Erotomanic Type/Grandiose Type/Jealous Type/Persecutory

	Type/Somatic Type/Mixed Type/Unspecified Type
298.8	Brief Psychotic Disorder

Specify if: With Marked Stressor(s)/Without Marked Stressor(s)/With Postpartum Onset

297.3	Shared Psychotic Disorder
293.xx	Psychotic Disorder Due to . . . [*Indicate the general medical condition*]
.81	With Delusions
.82	With Hallucinations
___.__	Substance-Induced Psychotic Disorder *(refer to Substance-Related Disorders for substance-specific codes)*

Specify if: With Onset During Intoxication/With Onset During Withdrawal

| 298.9 | Psychotic Disorder NOS |

Mood Disorders

Code current state of Major Depressive Disorder or Bipolar 1 Disorder in fifth digit:

1	Mild
2	Moderate
3	Severe Without Psychotic Features
4	Severe with Psychotic Features

Specify: Mood-Congruent Psychotic Features/Mood-Incongruent Psychotic Features

5	In Partial Remission
6	In Full Remission
0	Unspecified

The following specifiers apply (for current or most recent episodes) to Mood Disorders as noted:
[a]Severity/Psychotic/Remission Specifiers/[b]Chronic/[c]With Catatonic Features/[d]With Melancholic Features/[e]With Atypical Features/[f]With Postpartum Onset

The following specifiers apply to Mood Disorders as noted:
[g]With or Without Full Interepisode Recovery/[h]With Seasonal Pattern/[i]With Rapid Cycling

Depressive Disorders

296.xx	Major Depressive Disorder
.2x	Single Episode[a,b,c,d,e,f]
.3x	Recurrent[a,b,c,d,e,f,g,h]
300.4	Dysthymic Disorder

Specify if: Early Onset/Late Onset
Specify if: With Atypical Features

| 311 | Depressive Disorder NOS |

Bipolar Disorders

296.xx	Bipolar I Disorder
.0x	Single Manic Episode[a,c,f]
	Specify if: Mixed
.40	Most Recent Episode Hypomanic[g,h,i]
.4x	Most Recent Episode Manic[a,c,f,g,h,i]
.6x	Most Recent Episode Mixed[a,c,f,g,h,i]
.5x	Most Recent Episode Depressed[a,b,c,d,e,f,g,h,i]
.7	Most Recent Episode Unspecified[g,h,i]
296.89	Bipolar II Disorder[a,b,c,d,e,f,g,h,i]
	Specify (current or most recent episode): Hypomanic/Depressed
301.13	Cyclothymic Disorder
296.80	Bipolar Disorder NOS
293.83	Mood Disorder Due to . . . [*Indicate the general medical condition*]
	Specify type: With Depressive Features/With Major Depressive-Like Episode/With Manic Features/With Mixed Features
___.__	Substance-Induced Mood Disorder *(refer to Substance-Related Disorders for substance-specific codes)*
	Specify type: With Depressive Features/With Manic Features/With Mixed Features
	Specify if: With Onset During Intoxication/With Onset During Withdrawal
296.90	Mood Disorder NOS

Anxiety Disorders

300.01	Panic Disorder Without Agoraphobia
300.21	Panic Disorder With Agoraphobia
300.22	Agoraphobia Without History of Panic Disorder
300.29	Specific Phobia
	Specify type: Animal Type/Natural Environment Type/Blood-Injection-Injury Type/Situational Type/Other Type
300.23	Social Phobia
	Specify if: Generalized
300.3	Obsessive-Compulsive Disorder
	Specify if: With Poor Insight
309.81	Post-traumatic Stress Disorder
	Specify if: Acute/Chronic
	Specify if: With Delayed Onset
308.3	Acute Stress Disorder
300.02	Generalized Anxiety Disorder
293.89	Anxiety Disorder Due to . . . [*Indicate the general medical condition*]

Specify if: With Generalized Anxiety/With Panic Attacks/With Obsessive-Compulsive Symptoms

___.___ Substance-Induced Anxiety Disorder *(refer to Substance-Related Disorders for substance-specific codes)*

Specify if: With Generalized Anxiety/With Panic Attacks/With Obsessive-Compulsive Symptoms/With Phobic Symptoms

Specify if: With Onset During Intoxication/With Onset During Withdrawal

300.00 Anxiety Disorder NOS

Somatoform Disorders

300.81 Somatization Disorder
300.81 Undifferentiated Somatoform Disorder
300.11 Conversion Disorder
Specify type: With Motor Symptom or Deficit/With Sensory Symptom or Deficit/With Seizures or Convulsions/With Mixed Presentation
307.xx Pain Disorder
.80 Associated with Psychological Factors
.89 Associated with Both Psychological Factors and a General Medical Condition
Specify if: Acute/Chronic
300.7 Hypochondriasis
Specify if: With Poor Insight
300.81 Somatoform Disorder NOS

Factitious Disorders

300.xx Factitious Disorder
.16 With Predominantly Psychological Signs and Symptoms
.19 With Predominantly Physical Signs and Symptoms
.19 With Combined Psychological and Physical Signs and Symptoms
300.19 Factitious Disorder NOS

Dissociative Disorders

300.12 Dissociative Amnesia
300.13 Dissociative Fugue
300.14 Dissociative Identity Disorder
300.6 Depersonalization Disorder
300.15 Dissociative Disorder NOS

Sexual and Gender Identity Disorders

Sexual Dysfunctions

The following specifiers apply to all primary Sexual Dysfunctions:

Lifelong Type/Acquired Type

Generalized Type/Situational Type

Due to Psychological Factors/Due to Combined Factors

Sexual Desire Disorders

302.71   Hypoactive Sexual Desire Disorder

032.79   Sexual Aversion Disorder

Sexual Arousal Disorders

302.72   Female Sexual Arousal Disorder

302.72   Male Erectile Disorder

Orgasmic Disorders

302.73   Female Orgasmic Disorder

302.74   Male Orgasmic Disorder

302.75   Premature Ejaculation

Sexual Pain Disorders

302.76   Dyspareunia (Not Due to a General Medical Condition)

306.51   Vaginismus (Not Due to a General Medical Condition)

Sexual Dysfunction Due to a General Medical Condition

625.8   Female Hypoactive Sexual Desire Disorder Due to . . . [*Indicate the General Medical Condition*]

608.89   Male Hypoactive Sexual Desire Disorder Due to . . . [*Indicate the General Medical Condition*]

607.84   Male Erectile Disorder Due to . . . [*Indicate the General Medical Condition*]

625.0   Female Dyspareunia Due to . . . [*Indicate the General Medical Condition*]

608.89   Male Dyspareunia Due to . . . [*Indicate the General Medical Condition*]

625.8   Other Female Sexual Dysfunction Due to . . . [*Indicate the General Medical Condition*]

608.89   Other Male Sexual Dysfunction Due to . . . [*Indicate the General Medical Condition*]

___.___   Substance-Induced Sexual Dysfunction (Refer to Substance-Related Disorders for Substance-Specific Codes)

Specify if: With Impaired Desire/With Impaired Arousal/With Impaired Orgasm/With Sexual Pain

Specify if: With Onset During Intoxication

302.70 Sexual Dysfunction NOS

Paraphilias

302.4	Exhibitionism
302.81	Fetishism
302.89	Frotteurism
302.2	Pedophilia

Specify if: Sexually Attracted to Males/Sexually Attracted to Females/Sexually Attracted to Both

Specify if: Limited to Incest

Specify type: Exclusive Type/Nonexclusive Type

302.83	Sexual Masochism
302.84	Sexual Sadism
302.3	Transvestic Fetishism

Specify if: With Gender Dysphoria

302.82	Voyeurism
302.9	Paraphilia NOS

Gender Identity Disorders

302.xx	Gender Identity Disorder
.6	In Children
.85	In Adolescents or Adults

Specify if: Sexually Attracted to Males/Sexually Attracted to Females/Sexually Attracted to Both/Sexually Attracted to Neither

302.6	Gender Identity Disorder NOS
302.9	Sexual Disorder NOS

Eating Disorders

307.1	Anorexia Nervosa

Specify type: Restricting Type; Binge-Eating/Purging Type

307.51	Bulimia Nervosa

Specify type: Purging Type/Nonpurging Type

307.50	Eating Disorder NOS

Sleep Disorders

Primary Sleep Disorders

Dyssomnias

307.42	Primary Insomnia
307.44	Primary Hypersomnia
	Specify if: Recurrent
347	Narcolepsy
780.59	Breathing-Related Sleep Disorder
307.45	Circadian Rhythm Sleep Disorder
	Specify type: Delayed Sleep Phase Type/Jet Lag Type/Shift Work Type/Unspecified Type
307.47	Dyssomnia NOS

Parasomnias

307.47	Nightmare Disorder
307.46	Sleep Terror Disorder
307.46	Sleepwalking Disorder
307.47	Parasomnia NOS

Sleep Disorders Related to Another Mental Disorder

307.42	Insomnia Related to . . . [*Indicate the Axis I or Axis II Disorder*]
307.44	Hypersomnia Related to . . . [*Indicate the Axis I or Axis II Disorder*]

Other Sleep Disorders

780.xx	Sleep Disorder Due to . . . [*Indicate the General Medical Condition*]
.52	Insomnia Type
.54	Hypersomnia Type
.59	Parasomnia Type
.59	Mixed Type
___.__	Substance Induced Sleep Disorder *(Refer to Substance-Related Disorders for Substance-Specific Codes)*
	Specific type: Insomnia Type/Hypersomnia Type/Parasomnia Type/Mixed Type
	Specify if: With Onset During Intoxication/With Onset During Withdrawal

Impulse-Control Disorders Not Elsewhere Classified

312.34	Intermittent Explosive Disorder
312.32	Kleptomania
312.33	Pyromania
312.31	Pathological Gambling
312.39	Trichotillomania
312.30	Impulse-Control Disorder NOS

Adjustment Disorders

309.xx	Adjustment Disorder
.0	With Depressed Mood
.24	With Anxiety
.28	With Mixed Anxiety and Depressed Mood
.3	With Disturbance of Conduct
.4	With Mixed Disturbance of Emotions and Conduct
.9	Unspecified
	Specify if: Acute/Chronic

Personality Disorders

Note: These are coded on Axis II.

301.0	Paranoid Personality Disorder
301.20	Schizoid Personality Disorder
301.22	Schizotypal Personality Disorder
301.7	Antisocial Personality Disorder
301.83	Borderline Personality Disorder
301.50	Histrionic Personality Disorder
301.81	Narcissistic Personality Disorder
301.82	Avoidant Personality Disorder
301.6	Dependent Personality Disorder
301.4	Obsessive-Compulsive Personality Disorder
301.9	Personality Disorder NOS

Other Conditions That May Be a Focus of Clinical Attention

Psychological Factors Affecting Medical Condition

316	[*Specified Psychological Factor*] *Affecting* . . . [*Indicate the general medical condition*]
	Choose name based on nature of factors:
	Mental Disorder Affecting Medical Condition

Psychological Symptoms Affecting Medical Condition
Personality Traits or Coping Style Affecting Medical Condition
Maladaptive Health Behaviors Affecting Medical Condition
Stress-Related Physiological Response Affecting Medical Condition
Other or Unspecified Psychological Factors Affecting Medical Condition

Medication-Induced Movement Disorders

332.1	Neuroleptic-Induced Parkinsonism
333.92	Neuroleptic Malignant Syndrome
333.7	Neuroleptic-Induced Acute Dystonia
333.99	Neuroleptic-Induced Acute Akathisia
333.82	Neuroleptic-Induced Tardive Dyskinesia
333.1	Medication-Induced Postural Tremor
333.90	Medication-Induced Movement Disorder NOS

Other Medication-Induced Disorder

995.2	Adverse Effects of Medication NOS

Relational Problems

V61.9	Related Problem Related to a Mental Disorder or General Medical Condition
V61.20	Parent-Child Relational Problem
V61.1	Partner Relational Problem
V61.8	Sibling Relational Problem
V62.81	Relational Problem NOS

Problems Related to Abuse or Neglect

V61.21	Physical Abuse of Child *(Code 995.5 if Focus of Attention Is on Victim)*
V61.21	Sexual Abuse of Child *(Code 995.5 if Focus of Attention Is on Victim)*
V61.21	Neglect of Child *(Code 995.5 if Focus of Attention Is on Victim)*
V61.1	Physical Abuse of Adult *(Code 995.5 if Focus of Attention Is on Victim)*
V61.1	Sexual Abuse of Adult *(Code 995.5 if Focus of Attention Is on Victim)*

Additional Conditions That May Be a Focus of Clinical Attention

V15.81	Noncompliance with Treatment
V65.2	Malingering
V71.01	Adult Antisocial Behavior
V71.02	Child or Adolescent Antisocial Behavior
V62.89	Borderline Intellectual Functioning
	Note: This Is Coded on Axis II.
780.9	Age-Related Cognitive Decline
V62.82	Bereavement

V62.3	Academic Problem
V62.2	Occupational Problem
313.82	Identity Problem
V62.89	Religious or Spiritual Problem
V62.4	Acculturation Problem
V62.89	Phase of Life Problem

Additional Codes

300.9	Unspecified Mental Disorder (Nonpsychotic)
V71.09	No Diagnosis or Condition on Axis I
799.9	Diagnosis or Condition Deferred on Axis I
V71.09	No Diagnosis on Axis I
799.9	Diagnosis Deferred on Axis II

Multiaxial System

Axis I	Clinical Disorders
	Other Conditions That May Be a Focus of Clinical Attention
Axis II	Personality Disorders
	Mental Retardation
Axis III	General Medical Conditions
Axis IV	Psychosocial and Environmental Problems
Axis V	Global Assessment of Functioning

Emotional Factors with Physical Consequences

Emotional Problems Can Produce Physical Problems

While physical problems can cause emotional problems, the reverse also holds true. For example, stress seems to result in a general predisposition to illness. It can lead to various psycho-physiologic diseases (ulcers, colitis, high blood pressure). Persons who lead stressful lives and feel pressured by the constraints of time are prone to coronary artery disease. Of utmost importance is the fact that stress can deplete the neurotransmitters in the brain (norepinephrine, serotinin, dopamine) and thus in turn produce depression psychosis. Stress can also slow the speed of recovery from infectious disease or surgery. Loneliness may be an important factor in both the development of coronary artery disease and susceptibility to certain forms of cancer.

In addition, studies have shown that in the first year after the death of a close relative, there is a sevenfold increase in the mortality rate. (See the following outline of ways in which emotions influence the body.)

Emotional Factors with Physical Consequences

Unresolved emotional and spiritual problems can produce a host of physical problems. On the other hand, emotional well-being can promote physical health. Some of the more noteworthy ways in which emotions influence the body are suggested in the following outline.

1. When we are deprived of intimacy with others, our physical condition suffers.

a. In the first year after the death of a close relative, there is a sevenfold increase in the mortality rate (this is the conclusion of studies comparing the recently bereaved with the general population).

b. A young child separated from his mother for a prolonged period may fail to thrive and eventually die (anaclitic depression).

c. Research has shown that loneliness may be an important factor in both the development of coronary artery disease and susceptibility to cancer.

2. The presence of emotional stress has enormous (largely detrimental) effects on physical health.

a. Stress seems to result in a general predisposition to illness. It can also slow the speed of recovery from infectious diseases or surgery.

b. By virtue of the interplay between the psychological, nervous, and endocrine systems, stress can lower our resistance to infection:

stress
↓
depletion of norepinephrine
↓
irregularity in the secretion
of hypothalamic releasing factors
↓
change in the release of hormones
from the pituitary gland (e.g.,
growth hormones, luteinizing
hormones, thyroid-stimulating
hormone, adrenocorticotrophic
hormone, prolactin
↓
disturbances in endocrine glands

↓	↓
lowered resistance to physical diseases, including colds, pneumonia, cancer	increase in control ↓ increase in liver enzymes which deplete serotonin and norepinephrine. Also with increase in cortisol the body is on high alert status and that sustained high-alert status eventually produces disease in end organs. And finally, the high-sustained cortisol probably is a significant factor in eventual atrophy of

> the hippocampus that controls emotional
> memory, so with its atrophy one has
> a difficult time telling that the stress is
> over—the emotional pain continues even
> when the stress is gone.

Another result of the depletion of norepinephrine due to stress is physical and biochemical depression.

c. Stress plays a role in psychophysiologic diseases as well. Note once again the various parts of the body affected in the process.

stress
↓
hypothalamus
↓
brain stem
↓
autonomic nervous system
↓
pathology of various organs
(asthma, ulcers, colitis,
high blood pressure, rapid
heartbeat, anorexia nervosa)

d. "Type A" personalities (i.e., aggressive, time-conscious individuals who lead highly stressful lives) are prone to coronary artery disease.

e. If the stress is short-term and does not overwhelm the system, one beneficial effect is protection in times of danger. Under these circumstances stress results in the release of adrenaline and the "fight or flight" response.

3. A number of studies indicate that in the case of certain diseases, emotional factors may actually compound the physical symptoms brought on by physical causes.

a. In some circumstances placebos have been found to be between 30 and 60 percent as effective as active medication (regardless of the strength of the medication).

b. In some cases mock operation for arteriosclerotic heart disease may be as effective as actual bypass operations in reducing pain and increasing exercise toleration.

4. The emotional and spiritual dimensions of man can be utilized to promote physical health.

a. Once it was determined that the brain waves can be changed by imagining a pleasant experience (right cortex) or by intellectual exercise (left cortex), the next step was to teach people to exert control over illnesses through the supposedly involuntary nervous system (biofeedback). By the use of tension-sensitive instruments with graphic readouts, people have learned to control tension headaches, nocturnal tooth grinding, and cardiac arrhythmias. It is also possible to lower the heart rate, the respiration rate, oxygen consumption, and blood pressure.

b. Through faith and hope many people experience complete remission from what may have appeared to be physical problems.

RESOURCE F

Confidentiality Statement

Confidentiality is the cornerstone for building relationships. People will not confide in their mentor or counselor if they believe that information will be revealed to others. Therefore, be assured you can trust us.

We are bound by legal and ethical parameters when others (authorities and loved ones as appropriate) will be called. These are:

1. If a person is imminently suicidal.
2. If a person is homicidal.
3. If a minor is being abused physically or sexually.

RESOURCE G

Consent for Counseling/Mentoring

Many counselors/mentors today obtain a signed consent for counseling/mentoring. Here is an example. The particular form actually used could be individualized for the organization and the laws of the state. This is merely an example.

Consent for Counseling or Mentoring

For Adults/Minors 16 Years of Age or Older

In signing this consent, I am authorizing _____ to do counseling/mentoring as deemed necessary or advisable for the help in my condition. This consent is valid for each visit I make unless specifically revoked by me orally or in writing.

Name _____ Date _____

For Minors Under 16 Years of Age

In signing this consent, I am authorizing my child's counselor/mentor, _____, to do counseling/mentoring as deemed necessary or advisable for my child's condition. This consent is valid for each visit my child makes unless specifically revoked by me orally or in writing.

Name _____ Date _____

Daily Appointment Sheet

For: _____   Date: _____

8:00	_____
9:00	_____
10:00	_____
11:00	_____
12:00	_____
1:00	_____
2:00	_____
3:00	_____
4:00	_____
5:00	_____
6:00	_____
7:00	_____

RESOURCE I

Phone Message Form

Phone Message

DATE: _____ TIME: _____ FOR: _____

COUNSELEE'S NAME: _____

COUNSELEE'S PHONE NUMBER: (Home) _____ (Work)

_____

COMMENTS:

_____

_____

_____

_____

_____

_____

_____

_____

_____

                                    STAFF: _____

Release of Information Form

At times a counselor or mentor may need to confer with a colleague (medical doctor, therapist, pastor, etc.). Legally, it is important to receive permission and documentation of that permission. The following is an example of such a release of information form. Any such form needs to be adapted to the particular needs of the organization and the laws of the state and is given here only as an example of one such form.

Authorization for Release of Information

I hereby authorize _____ and _____ to exchange any and all information pertinent to my condition.

By signing this consent to release information, I agree not to hold liable either party above as they discuss my case with each other.

Name _____ Date _____

Examples of Brochures

Example 1

We have included a copy of the clinic's brochure for you to use as a guideline in designing your brochure. Your brochure will need to be tailored toward your ministry.

THE

MINIRTH

CLINIC

A

Matter

Of

Caring

Mental health problems now affect more Americans than ever. Because emotional stress is a part of everyday life, the MINIRTH CLINIC is dedicated to confronting these problems with practical, realistic solutions.

The Minirth Clinic has a commitment to excellence in many areas: maintaining a professional staff; compassionate, individualized patient care; and comprehensive, quality treatment programs and services.

Through our medical and counseling practice and outreach programs, the staff maintains a conviction that the most effective way of helping an individual with emotional problems is by treating the person as a whole.

For positive changes in your life . . .

The psychiatrists, psychologists, family therapists, licensed professional counselors, and social workers are dedicated to helping people find lasting peace and balanced lives.

Medical Management

The physicians trained in psychiatry recognize and recommend treatment for those patients whose emotional symptoms stem from a medical dimension. New psychiatric medication can make a dramatic difference for many individuals.

Individual Counseling

The goal for each patient is positive personality growth, the development of problem-solving and decision-making abilities, and the development of coping skills.

Marriage and Family Counseling

Learning more effective communication and interaction styles equips families and couples to develop healthier, more positive relationships.

Child and Adolescent Services

The Clinic offers specialized programs to meet the needs of troubled young people who are experiencing emotional, psychological, family, and social distress.

Our professional staff provides a variety of services for young people. We use a variety of methods to develop treatment programs that promote growth and change, positive relationships, personal values, and acceptable behavioral patterns.

Group Counseling

Participants have the opportunity to explore their feelings and to discuss problems with peers who are struggling with similar issues. The environment is supportive where confidentiality and beliefs are respected. This interaction helps each person gain new insights and perspectives.

Assessment and Diagnostic Services

Comprehensive evaluations may include confidential clinical interviews as well as appropriate psychological, developmental, personality, neuropsychological, intellectual, medical, and laboratory testing. Results help determine appropriate methods of treatment for a patient. Also extensive mental health wellness evaluations are available.

Fees

Psychiatrist (M.D.)
Initial visit
Follow-up
Therapist (Ph.D)
Initial visit
Follow-up
Therapist (M.A.)
Initial visit
Follow-up

We also have LPC-interns and practicum students with lower fees.

Note: Cancellation of appointments must be made at least twenty-four hours in advance, or the patient will be subject to a charge.

Hours

Our psychiatrists and a number of our therapists maintain some evening and Saturday hours to avoid necessity of missing work or school.

Prescriptions

Psychiatrists on staff prescribe medication and provide medication management as needed.

Emergencies

An answering service is available for all calls after office hours.

Insurance

The Clinic is committed to providing the optimum level of patient care at an affordable cost. Many major insurance carriers will cover patient counseling services. Our clinic will provide a form at the end of each visit which the client can submit to the insurance company. We ask that clients pay at the time of their visit, unless prior arrangements have been made.

Managed Care

The Clinic provides quality and affordable counseling services to employees and families of business and industries through specific contract arrangements.

Confidentiality

Confidentiality is strictly maintained. No information about a patient is released without the patient's written consent.

RADIO/INTERNET

Dr. Minirth can be heard Saturday's at 1:00 pm CST on KLIF (570AM), and Thursday evenings on the WORD (100.7FM). Please visit our Web site at www.minirthclinic.com.

SELF-HELP BOOKS

Clinic doctors and therapists have written numerous self-help books dealing with a variety of life's issues. These books are available from your local bookstore.

SPEAKERS' BUREAU
AND WORKSHOPS
"Speaking of Mental Health . . ."

The Clinic's professional staff is available to speak to churches, schools, clubs, businesses, and community organizations. These presentations are not only informative and emotionally uplifting; they may also be a catalyst for positive growth in your life. THE MINIRTH CLINIC is dedicated to

- *reverence for each person's worth and dignity*

- *renewing hope and peace*

- *the matter of caring*

"What James Dobson became to the family, Frank Minirth became to Christian Counseling." —J. Allen Peterson

- Medical Management

- Specialized Mental Health Care Services

- Comprehensive Assessment and Treatment Programs

- Individualized Services

- Distinctive Counseling Philosophy

- Compassionate, Confidential Care

- Commitment to Excellence

- Mental Health Wellness Evaluations

The Minirth Clinic, P.A.
2301 N. Greenville Ave.
Suite 200
Richardson, Texas 75080
Phone (972) 669-1733
(888) 646-4784
Fax (972) 669-1403

Example 2

This brochure is more of a generic Christian counseling brochure.

John Doe
Center for Christian Care

Our purpose is to meet the needs of the body of Christ through helping believers deal with their issues so they can be more effective workers in the kingdom of Christ.

The main avenue to accomplish the purpose and mission of this ministry is to make available appropriate, Christ-centered counseling or mentoring.

Enrichment opportunities

Just as in any war, there are causalities. We care for the wounded and restore them so they continue to minister to this world.

Our Staff

John Doe
Center for Christian Care

Secondary Business Address
Your Address Line 2
Your Address Line 3
Your Address Line 4

Phone: 555-555-5555
Fax: 555-555-5555
E-mail:

Build up, build up, prepare the road! Remove the obstacles out of the way of my people (Isa. 57:14, NIV).

Tel: 555-555-5555

Family & Personal Care

The Bible recommends that we seek out the counsel of wise, experienced, and God-honoring counselors. John Doe Center for Christian Care provides this wise and godly counsel.

We provide Christ-centered professional Christian care and mentoring. Both male and female licensed counselors are available.

At the Center for Christian Care, we seek to minister to the whole person—spiritually, emotionally, and psychologically, through biblical counsel.

Marriage and Family

We offer a confidential setting in which individuals and couples can openly discuss feelings and problems and work toward solving difficulties.

Care includes:

- those experiencing grief and loss

- those experiencing separation or divorce

- those in life transitions

Premarital
Defining expectations:

- sexual intimacy

- budget and finances

- handling conflict

- loving, serving, and caring for each other

Group and Special Needs
Small groups are offered for addictions, codependency, trauma resolution, grief recovery, and more. These groups, as well as seminars for issues such as parenting, stress management, and communication skills, are offered on a semester format.

Personal
Handling depression; improving your self-image; and solving career-related difficulties.

"We proclaim him, admonishing and teaching everyone with all wisdom, so that we may present everyone perfect in Christ" (Col. 1:28 NIV).

In our fast-paced world, it feels great to have someone who will:

- Really listen

- Take time to care

- See you through a tough time

- Provide encouragement instead of advice

- Be a loving, caring friend

- Faithfully pray for you

John Doe
Center for Christian Counseling

Secondary Business Address
Your Address Line 2
Your Address Line 3
Your Address Line 4

Phone: 555-555-5555
Fax: 555-555-5555
Email:

Examples of Letterheads

Example 1
Frank B. Minirth, Ph.D., M.D.
Diplomate, American Board of Psychiatry & Neurology
Diplomate, American Board of Forensic Medicine
2301 N. Greenville Ave., Suite 200
Richardson, Texas 75082
(972) 669-1733

The
Minirth
Clinic

A
Matter
Of
Caring

Example 2

MINIRTH CLINIC, P.A.
2301 N. Greenville Ave., Suite 200
Richardson, Texas 75082
Telephone: 972-669-1733 Fax: 972-669-1403

Child and Adolescent Services   **Children, Adolescents and Young Adults**

TERRY J. MOODY, Ph.D., DABPS
Child and Adolescent Psychologist
Director of Child and Adolescent Services
Diplomate, American Board of Psychological Specialties

Example 3

The Minirth Clinic | *A Matter Of Caring*

Officers
Frank Minirth, Ph.D., M.D.
President

Directors
Mary Alice Minirth,
Sr. Executive Director
Vickie Gage,
Executive Director

Psychiatrists
Frank Minirth, M.D.
Noe Neaves, M.D.

Medical Personnel
V. Neal, R.N., N.P., Ph.D.
Linda Behrendt, R.N.

Psychotherapists
Harry Beverly, Ph.D., LPC
Les Carter, Ph.D., LPC
Traci Davis, LPC
Ann Epps, Ph.D., LPC
Brad Fairchild, LPC
Stacey Farmer, LPC
Terri Fusilier, LPC
Robert Holmes, Ph.D.
Ann Key, LPC
Terry Moody, Ph.D.
Murriel Schulte, Ph.D.
Carol Speckman, LPC
Keith Wright, Ph.D.
S. Zakhary, LMSW, A.C.P., CADAC

2301 N. Greenville Ave. Ste #200 Richardson, Tx. 75082
Phone 972-669-1733
Fax 972-669-1403
E-mail: staff@minirthclinic.com
Visit our Web page: www.minirthclinic.com

Mental Evaluations and Progress Notes

Christian counselors often need models of mental evaluations and progress notes. These are included in the following pages.

Example 1
A Less Detailed Initial Information Form

Initial Information Form—Your Life in Review

Name: _____   Date: _____

I. PRESENTING PICTURE (An overview of why you are here, with chief concern and any symptoms):

_____

_____

_____

_____

_____

_____

_____

_____

_____

II. PAST HISTORY (An overview of your life from birth until now):

_____
_____
_____
_____
_____
_____
_____
_____
_____
_____

III. CURRENT LIFE (An overview of what your support system is and what your life revolves around now):

_____
_____
_____
_____
_____
_____
_____
_____
_____
_____
_____

Example 2
A More Detailed Initial Information Form

Initial Information Form—Your Life in Review

Please take a few moments to fill out this form as complete as possible. From this history, valuable information may be realized by examining areas such as the PRESENTING PICTURE (current symptoms and what precipitated them); the HISTORY OF PRESENT PROBLEMS (current symptoms); the PAST HISTORY (past issues that may be important now); and the DYNAMIC FORMULATION (your own attempt to pull all of this information together). In brief, this is what your life has been. You can work toward changing it to what you want it to be.

Name: _____ Date: _____

Briefly describe why you are here. _____

I. PRESENTING PICTURE (**Current symptoms and what precipitated them**) I am a ____ year old ☐ [M] or ☐ [F] from _____ (city). If I had to describe my one major symptom, it would be ☐ Depression ☐ Anxiety ☐ Obsessive Worries ☐ Panic Anxiety ☐ Times of Confusion ☐ Drug Abuse ☐ Inattention/ Hyperactivity ☐ Mood Swings ☐ Loss of Memory ☐ Other _____ (name). The major stressor(s) that precipitated my symptom is/are ☐ Marital Issues ☐ Parent/Child Issues ☐ Job Issues ☐ Health Issues ☐ Relationship Issues ☐ Financial Issues ☐ Issues of Past (☐ Guilt ☐ Abuse ☐ Family of Origin) ☐ Other _____ (name). My symptom(s) began: _____ (date). My symptom(s) increased: _____ (date). My three biggest worries in life at the present time are: 1. _____ 2. _____
3. _____

I am currently taking the following prescribed psychiatric medications:

Medicine & Dosage	DATE BEGAN	SIDE EFFECTS	RESULTS

I am currently taking the following prescribed general medications: _____

II. HISTORY OF PRESENT PROBLEM: (Current symptoms: Check all that apply)

Occ'l Wkly Daily

Depression & Anxiety
☐ ☐ ☐ Increased crying
☐ ☐ ☐ Sad mood
☐ ☐ ☐ Lack of motivation
☐ ☐ ☐ Poor concentration
☐ ☐ ☐ Sleep Pattern (More) or (Less)
☐ ☐ ☐ Appetite changes • or •
☐ ☐ ☐ Weight changes • or •
☐ ☐ ☐ Lack of interest
☐ ☐ ☐ Decreased self-esteem
☐ ☐ ☐ Sad affect
☐ ☐ ☐ Hopeless/Helpless feeling

Occ'l Wkly Daily

Depression & Anxiety
☐ ☐ ☐ Nightmares
☐ ☐ ☐ Other: _____

OTHER SYMPTOMS
☐ ☐ ☐ *Inattention*
☐ ☐ ☐ Hyperactivity
☐ ☐ ☐ Delusions/Paranoia
☐ ☐ ☐ Hallucinations (hearing voices/music that no one else hears)
☐ ☐ ☐ High with racing thoughts, increased speech, decreased sleep, and increased

activity

☐	☐	☐	Energy level • or •	☐	☐	☐	Isolating self from all contact with others
☐	☐	☐	Chest discomfort	☐	☐	☐	Amnesia
☐	☐	☐	Abdominal (Stomach) distress	☐	☐	☐	Running away
☐	☐	☐	Feeling dizzy	☐	☐	☐	Truancy
☐	☐	☐	Fear of going crazy	☐	☐	☐	Memory impaired with trouble organizing and sequencing
☐	☐	☐	Startled response				
☐	☐	☐	Chills or hot flashes	☐	☐	☐	Somatization—undue health worries with no adequate medical explanation
☐	☐	☐	Outburst of anger				
☐	☐	☐	Anxiety in general	☐	☐	☐	Agitated—irritable (easily annoyed and provoked to anger)
☐	☐	☐	Restlessness, keyed up, fatigued, decreased concentration, irritability, muscle tension, decreased sleep				
				☐	☐	☐	Drugs you've used: _____
☐	☐	☐	Hypervigilance—excessive attention and focus on all internal and external stimuli	☐	☐	☐	Behavioral problems—Name: _____ _____
☐	☐	☐	Obsessions/compulsions—constant checking, washing, or counting type behaviors; unrelenting worries	☐	☐	☐	Developmental problems—Name: _____ _____ _____
☐	☐	☐	Avoidance of stimuli associated with a trauma	☐	☐	☐	Self-mutilation—Name: _____
☐	☐	☐	Agoraphobia—anxiety of places or inescapable situations	☐	☐	☐	Legal Issues—Name: _____
☐	☐	☐	Specific phobia—marked and persistent fear of certain objects or situations	☐	☐	☐	Sexual Issues—Name: _____
☐	☐	☐	Social phobia—marked and persistent fear of social or performance situations where embarrassment may occur	☐	☐	☐	Eating Issues—Name: _____
				☐	☐	☐	Impulsive
☐	☐	☐	Post-traumatic stress experiences	☐	☐	☐	Aphasia, apraxia, agnosia
☐	☐	☐	Intense fear	☐	☐	☐	Disturbance of executive functioning
☐	☐	☐	Rapid heartbeat	☐	☐	☐	Suspicious
☐	☐	☐	Increased sweating				
☐	☐	☐	Shortness of breath				
☐	☐	☐	Withdrawn				

III. PAST HISTORY: (Past issues that may be important now)

A. Have you had similar and significant symptom(s) in the past? ☐ Yes ☐ No. If yes, when: _____

Did they recently increase? ☐ Yes ☐ No. If yes, what caused the increase? _____

B. Name three past stressful events in your life that precipitated the original symptom(s): _____

_____

C. Prior psychiatric hospitalization? ☐ Yes ☐ No. If yes, where: _____

Reason hospitalized: _____

Prior outpatient counseling: ☐ Yes ☐ No. If yes, therapist(s)/date(s): _____

D. Substance abuse history. ☐ Yes ☐ No. If yes, when did it begin? _____

Substances _____

Drug(s) of choice: _____ Any treatment ☐ Yes ☐ No Date(s): _____

E. Brief medical history _____

F. Any known allergies _____

G. Past psychiatric medications: _____

Medicine & Dosage	YEAR GIVEN	SIDE EFFECTS	RESULTS

H. Family of origin issues:

   1. Father—what was he like? _____

   2. Mother—what was she like? _____

   3. Brothers/Sisters—how many of each? _____

   4. Where did you fit in birth order? _____

   5. What type of relationship did you have with your sibling(s)? _____

   6. School history—what type of grades? _____ How many years? _____

   7. Marriages—how many? _____ What types of stress in each marriage? _____

   8. Children—how many? _____ Ages and sex of each? _____

I. My childhood overall was: ☐ Painful ☐ Uneventful ☐ Good   Birth and early development was ☐ Normal ☐ Abnormal

J. History of: ☐ Abuse ☐ School problems ☐ Abandonment ☐ Relationship problems ☐ Disability ☐ Job problems ☐ Legal ☐ Other (Name) _____

K. I presently live: ☐ Alone ☐ With spouse ☐ With parents ☐ Other _____
My current support system is ☐ Good ☐ Fair ☐ Poor

L. Psychiatric history— Name(s) of past psychiatrist(s) and/or therapist(s) _____

M. Job history and current job _____

N. Religious history _____

O. Name of referral source to the clinic _____

P. Past and current history summary: I grew up in _____ (state). I grew up in the ☐ country ☐ a small town ☐ a large city. Both parents ☐ were ☐ were not in the home. I was one of _____ children and was _____ in the birth order. My childhood was ☐ good ☐ difficult ☐ very difficult in the sense of _____. In high school my life revolved around ☐ sports ☐ work ☐ church ☐ social ☐ academics ☐ other _____ (name). After high school I ☐ did ☐ did not attend college. After high school, life has been ☐ good ☐ difficult ☐ very difficult in the sense of _____. I am currently ☐ single ☐ married for _____ years. I presently live ☐ alone ☐ with spouse ☐ with parents ☐ Other _____. My current support system is ☐ good ☐ fair ☐ poor. I have been married _____ time(s). I ☐ do not have ☐ do have _____ (number) of children. I ☐ do not have ☐ do have health problems. (List any, past or present, problems: _____.) Life now centers around ☐ family ☐ work ☐ friends ☐ other _____. Recently life has been ☐ good ☐ difficult ☐ very difficult in the sense of _____.

IV. DYNAMIC FORMULATION: (Putting it all together). Several factors may be involved in why I am in my current state of mind. First a CURRENT STRESSFUL LIFE EVENT of ☐ relationship issue(s) ☐ job/school issue(s) ☐ health issue(s) ☐ financial issue(s) ☐ other _____ (name).

Second, under stress I tend to turn to the DEFENSE MECHANISM of ☐ introjection of my emotions ☐ denial of my emotions ☐ suppression/repression of emotions ☐ acting out ☐ rationalization ☐ projection of my emotions onto others ☐ undue health worries ☐ withdrawal into my own world ☐ passive behavior ☐ other defenses of _____ (name) with my PERSONALITY of being ☐ perfectionistic ☐ emotional ☐ suspicious ☐ idealizing, then devaluating others ☐ having few or no friends ☐ living in my own world ☐ low self-confidence ☐ self-centered ☐ eccentric ☐ withdrawn and depressed ☐ alternating moods from high to low ☐ other personality issue(s) _____.

Third, my EARLY LIFE is an important factor in that it was ☐ good ☐ difficult ☐ very difficult with ☐ abuse issue(s) of some kind (verbal, physical, sexual) ☐ abandonment issue(s) ☐ self-image issue(s) ☐ other issue(s)
_____(name).

Fourthly, GENETIC FACTORS ☐ do not seem to contribute ☐ do seem to contribute in that a relative of mine _____ (name) had _____.

In spite of all of the above, my SPIRITUAL LIFE ☐ has ☐ has not been a factor it seems in the sense of _____. By putting all of the above together, insight into my life may emerge.

Example 3
A Less Detailed Mental Evaluation

Mental Evaluation

NAME: _____ DATE: _____

I. PRESENTING PICTURE (SEE INITIAL SCREENING QUESTIONNAIRE):

_____

_____

_____

_____

_____

II. HISTORY OF PRESENT PROBLEM (SEE INITIAL SCREENING QUESTIONNAIRE):

_____

_____

_____

_____

_____

III. PAST HISTORY (SEE INITIAL SCREENING QUESTIONNAIRE):

_____

_____

_____

_____

_____

IV. MENTAL EXAMINATION

A. ATTENTION TO APPEARANCE: □ Very Good □ Good □ Fair □ Poor
COOPERATION: □ Good □ Fair □ Poor   MOTOR ACTIVITY: □ Agitated □ Normal □ Retarded
COMFORT/STYLE: □ Open □ Guarded □ Inhibited □ Impoverished □ Obsessive □ Obtuse
STATED AGE: Appears □ Older □ Younger □ Stated age □ SPEECH RATE: □ Rapid □ Normal
□ Slow

B. INTELLECTUAL FUNCTIONING:
□ Oriented to person, place, time □ Intact in general □ Adequate knowledge of general info
□ Memory, recent and remote intact
□ IQ estimated _____ Other _____ □ Serial 7's from 100 □ Divide 100 by 7's
□ Ability to recall four objects after two min. □ Abstraction

C. COMMUNICATION: ☐ Logical ☐ Rational ☐ Coherent ☐ Other _____

D. THOUGHT PROCESSES: ☐ Associations Approp. ☐ Loose ☐ Bizarre ☐ Flight of Ideas

E. AFFECT: ☐ Sad ☐ Flat ☐ Anxious ☐ WNL

F. MOOD/AFFECT: ☐ Euthymic ☐ Depressed ☐ Euphoric ☐ Irritable ☐ Anxious ☐ Labile
☐ Inappropriate

G. RANGE OF AFFECT: ☐ Wide ☐ Normal ☐ Affected ☐ Flat

H. INSIGHT & JUDGMENT: ☐ Good ☐ Fair ☐ Poor

V. DIAGNOSIS

AXIS I: Primary Diagnosis and Code: _____

AXIS II: Personality Traits/Disorder: _____

AXIS III: Related Medical Issues: _____

AXIS IV: Stressors: Type _____
and Severity (☐ mild, ☐ moderate, ☐ severe)

AXIS V: GAF: _____

VI. GOALS INCLUDE

☐ Decrease intensity of symptoms

☐ Increase level of functioning

☐ Improved Behavioral Manifestations

☐ Other _____

VII. TREATMENT PLAN

A. PSYCHOTHERAPY: _____

B. PSYCHOPHARMACOLOGY

1. Labs   ☐ Ordered ☐ Requested Previous Labs

2. Meds—Informed of the side effects of MEDS - ☐ HANDOUTS given

MEDICINE & DOSAGE

_____   _____

_____   _____

C. PSYCHOSOCIAL AND OTHER

1. Suicide contract ☐ Yes ☐ No ☐ N/A

2. Other _____

VIII. PROGNOSIS ☐ Good ☐ Fair ☐ Poor ☐ Guarded

IX. SUMMARY _____

_____

_____

_____

_____

_____

_____

_____   _____
Return Date   Signature

Example 4
A More Detailed Mental Evaluation

Mental Evaluation

Name: _____ Date: _____ BP: _____ WT: _____ HT: _____

I. PRESENTING PICTURE: This is a ____ year old M__ F__ with the chief complaint of " _____."
The major stressor(s) that precipitated this symptom is/are: _____.

II. HISTORY OF PRESENT PROBLEM: This patient presented with the following symptoms:

A. Depression/Anxiety Symptoms (see INITIAL INFORMATION FORM)

> **SUICDIAL**
> Passing Thoughts ____ Serious Consider ____
> Plan ____ Attempt ____

☐ Increased crying　　　☐ Abdominal (stomach) distress　　☐ Startled response　　　☐ Fear of going crazy

☐ Sad mood　　　　　　☐ Outbursts of anger　　　　　☐ Avoidance of stimuli associated　☐ Intense fear

☐ Lack of motivation　　☐ Anxiety in general　　　　　　with a trauma　　　　　　☐ Rapid heartbeat

☐ Poor concentration　　☐ Restless, keyed up, fatigued,　☐ Post-traumatic stress experience　☐ Chills or hot flashes

☐ Energy (more) or (less)　　decreased concentration, irritability,　☐ Obsessions/Compulsions—constant　☐ Increased sweating

☐ Sleep pattern (more) or (less)　muscle tension, decreased sleep　checking, washing, or counting type　☐ Trembllng

☐ Appetite changes (more) or (less)　☐ Hypervigilance—excessive attention　behaviors; unrelenting worries　☐ Shortness of breath

☐ Weight changes (more) or (less)　and focus on all internal/external　☐ Specific phobia—marked and　☐ Withdrawn

☐ Lack of interest　　　stimuli　　　　　　　　persistent fear of certain objects　☐ Nightmares

☐ Decreased Self-Esteem　☐ Feeling dizzy　　　　　　or situations　　　　　　☐ Other _____

B. Attention Deficit Disorder Symptoms: ☐ Inattention ☐ Hyperactivity ☐ Impairment Functionally at: ____

C. Psychotic-like Symptoms: ☐ Hallucinations ☐ Delusions ☐ Paranoia ☐ Flat/Inappropriate Affect
☐ Loose association ☐ Withdrawn ☐ Bizarre behavior

D. Manic Symptoms: ☐ Increased speech ☐ Decreased judgment ☐ Increased grandiosity ☐ Decreased sleep
☐ Increased Energy ☐ Flight of ideas ☐ Racing thoughts

E. Other Symptoms: ☐ Somatization ☐ Substance abuse or dependence (drug) _____
☐ Agitated ☐ Aggressive/assaultive ☐ Isolative ☐ Truancy ☐ Running away ☐ Suspicious ☐ Withdrawn
☐ Nonfunctional

F. Organicity: ☐ Decreased memory ☐ Labile affect ☐ Decreased intellectual functioning
☐ Decreased judgment

G. Impulse Control Issues: ☐ Gambling ☐ Trichotillomania

H. Other: ☐ Legal issues ☐ Sexual dysfunctions ☐ Eating issues ☐ Dissociative state ☐ Self-mutilation
☐ Homicidal Family Psychiatric History _____

III. PAST HISTORY: (see INITIAL INFORMATION FORM): A. Symptom onset: _____
(Date) Symptom Increased: _____ (Date)

B. Precipitating Stressors _____

C. Prior Psychiatric Hospitalization? ☐ Yes ☐ No reason hospitalized: _____

Location/Dates _____ Location/Dates _____

Prior Outpatient Counseling ☐ Yes ☐ No Therapist/Date _____ Therapist/Date _____

D. Substance Abuse History ☐ Yes ☐ No Onset _____ Substances _____

   Previous Treatment _____

E. Brief Medical History: _____

F. Describe Any Known Allergies: _____

G. Past Psychiatric Meds: _____

H. Current Meds: a. Psychiatric _____ b. Other _____

I. The Patient's Childhood Overall Was ☐ Good ☐ Uneventful ☐ Painful in the sense of _____

J. History of: ☐ Abuse ☐ School Problems ☐ Abandonment ☐ Relationship Problems ☐ Disability

   ☐ Job Problems ☐ Legal Problems ☐ Drugs

K. Current Resides: ☐ Alone ☐ With Spouse ☐ With Parents ☐ Other

   _____ Current Support System: ☐ Good ☐ Fair ☐ Poor

L. Summary: _____

   _____

   _____

M. Current Job: _____

IV. MENTAL EXAMINATION: A. Appearance: ☐ *Attention to Appearance:* ☐ Very good ☐ Good ☐ Fair ☐ Poor

   _____ ☐ *Motor Activity:* ☐ Agitated ☐ Normal ☐ Retarded

   ☐ *Cooperation:* ☐ Good ☐ Fair ☐ Poor ☐ *Comfort/Style:* ☐ Open ☐ Guarded ☐ Inhibited ☐ Impoverished

   ☐ Obsessive ☐ Obtuse

   ☐ *Stated Age — Patient Appears:* ☐ Older ☐ Younger ☐ Stated Age ☐ *Speech Rate:* ☐ Rapid ☐ Normal

   ☐ Slow

B. Intellectual Functioning: ☐ Oriented to person, place, time ☐ Intact in general ☐ Adequate knowledge of

   general information ☐ Memory, recent and remote intact ☐ IQ estimated ☐ Serial 7s from 100 ☐ 100

   divided by 7s ☐ Ability to recall 4 objects after 2 minutes ☐ Abstraction ☐ Other _____

C. Communication: ☐ Logical ☐ Rational ☐ Coherent ☐ Other _____

D. Thought Processes: ☐ Associations appropriate ☐ Loose ☐ Bizarre ☐ Flight of ideas

E. Mood Affect: ☐ *Mood:* ☐ Euthymic ☐ Depressed ☐ Euphoric ☐ Irritable ☐ Anxious ☐ Labile

   ☐ Inappropriate ☐ *Affect:* ☐ Sad ☐ Flat ☐ Anxious ☐ WNL

      ☐ *Range of Affect:* ☐ Wide ☐ Normal ☐ Affected ☐ Flat   **VI. TREATMENT PLAN**:

F. Insight and Judgment: ☐ Good ☐ Fair ☐ Poor   A. Psychotherapy _____

G. Impulse Control: ☐ Good ☐ Fair ☐ Poor   B. Psychopharmacology

V. DIAGNOSIS: 1. Meds _____

   Axis I   Primary Diagnosis and Code _____ _____   _____

   Axis II   Personality Traits/Disorders _____ _____   2. Labs Ordered _____

   Axis III   Related Medical Issues   _____ _____   3. Told of range of side effects of

                                   meds?

   Axis IV   Stressors: Type/Severity   _____ _____   4. Handouts Given _____

            (mild, moderate, severe)   C. Psychosocial and Other: _____

Axis V   GAF   _____   ☐ *Suicide Contract?* ☐ No ☐ Yes ☐ NA

VII.   GOALS INCLUDE: ☐ Decrease intensity of symptoms ☐ Improved behavioral manifestations
☐ Improved Functioning

VIII. PROGNOSIS: ☐ Good ☐ Fair ☐ Poor ☐ Guarded

EVALUATIONS DONE TODAY OR REQUESTED Self Report on Scale of 0–10 (10 being worse)

☐ Psychiatric Evaluation	1. Depression _____	9. Behavior Problems _____
☐ Life History Evaluation	2. Anxiety _____	10. Hyperactivity _____
☐ Panic Evaluation	3. Insomnia _____	11. OCD _____
☐ ADHD Rating Scale/Checklist	4. Low Energy _____	12. Low Functioning _____
☐ Neurological	5. Anger _____	13. Dysthymia _____
☐ Bipolar ☐ 6. Beck Depression (BDI)	6. Low Motivation _____	14. Stressor Severity _____
☐ OppDD ☐ Beck Anxiety (BAI)	7. Manic _____	15. Confusion _____
	8. Inattention _____	16. Worry _____
		17. Pain _____

SUMMARY _____

_____

_____

_____   _____

       Return Date   **Signature**

Example 5
A Less Detailed Progress Note

Progress Notes

Name of Patient: _____ Date: _____

1. Diagnosis
   AXIS I: Primary Diagnosis & Code: _____
   AXIS II: Personality Traits/Disorder: _____
   AXIS III: Related Medical Issues: _____
   AXIS IV: Stressors: Type & Severity (mild, moderate, severe):   _____
   AXIS V: Current GAF: _____

2. Topics Discussed (circle please)
   a. Current stressors   f. Abuse issues   k. Past
   b. Losses   g. Abandonment issues   l. Guilt
   c. Marital issues   h. Health issues   m. Family of origin
   d. Parent/child issues   i. Financial worries or issues   n. Other/or extra
   e. Job/school issues   j. Medicines   details:_____

3. Suicidal _____ Yes _____ No _____ No-Suicide Contract done _____

4. Current Status: Improved _____ Same _____ Worse _____

5. Goals: 1. Decreased intensity of symptoms
               2. Increased level of function
               3. Improved behavioral manifestations
               4. Other _____

6. Comments:

   _____
   _____
   _____
   _____
   _____

7. Return: _____

_____
Therapist

Example 6
A More Detailed Progress Note

PROGRESS NOTES FOR PSYCHIATRISTS

Name of Patient: _____   Date: _____

Diagnosis: _____   Current GAF: _____

On a scale of 0–10, with "10" being the *worst*, where are you today?

1. Depression	_____	10. Hyperactivity	_____
2. Anxiety	_____	11. OCD	_____
3. Insomnia	_____	12. Low function	_____
4. Low energy	_____	13. Dysthymia	_____
5. Anger	_____	14. Stressor severity	_____
6. Low motivation	_____	15. Confusion	_____
7. Manic	_____	16. Worry	_____
8. Inattention	_____	17. Pain	_____
9. Behavior prob.	_____		

---

1. Current Status: Improved _____ Same _____ Worse _____

2. Topics discussed (circle please):

A. Current stressors	G. Abandonment issues	L. Social issues	Q. _____Issues of:
B. Losses	H. Health issues	M. Relationship issues	
C. Marital issues	I. Financial worries or issues	N. Family issues	☐ past
D. Parent/child issues	J. Medicines	O. Current behavioral	☐ abandonment
E. Job/school issues	K. Other/additional details	improvements	☐ guilt
F. "Abuse" issues	_____	P. Plans in near future	☐ family of origin

3. History Reviewed: Focused _____   Expanded _____   Detailed _____   Comprehensive _____

4. Examination (Evaluation): Focused _____ Expanded _____   Detailed _____   Comprehensive _____

5. Decision Making: Straightforward _____   Low Complexity _____   Moderate _____
   Complexity _____

6. A. Psychopharmacology: ☐ Told patient about the range of side effects of MEDS   ☐ Handouts given
   Current Medications: Changes:

   1. _____   _____   _____
   2. _____   _____   _____
   3. _____   _____   _____
   4. _____   _____   _____
   5. _____   _____   _____
   6. _____   _____   _____

B. Psychotherapy:

   1. Continue Psychotherapy: Yes _____ No _____   Therapist _____

2. Comment: _____

C. Psychosocial:

   Comment, if pertinent: _____

7. Return date: _____

8. Lab: _____

9. Suicidal _____ Patient agreed to a "No Suicide Contract" _____ Not Suicidal _____

10. Affect: _____

11. Symptoms today: _____

12. Side effects of medication: _____

13. Biggest issues of concern today that need to be changed, in order: _____
_____

14. Summary: _____
_____
_____

15. Goals: A. Decrease of Symptoms   B. Increase of Functioning   C. Improved Behavioral Manifestations
   D. Other: _____

16. Prognosis: A. Good _____ B. Fair _____ C. Poor _____ D. Guarded _____

      _____   _____

           Return Date   **Signature**

RESOURCE N

Examples of
Various Business Cards

THE MINIRTH CLINIC
A Matter Of Caring

VIRGINIA NEAL, Ph.D., ANP, MSCP
Clinical Psychopharmacologist, Licensed Psychologist, Advanced Nurse Practitioner

THE MINIRTH CLINIC
Phone: 972/669-1733
Fax: 972/669-1403

2301 N. Greenville Avenue #200
Richardson, Texas 75082

THE MINIRTH CLINIC
A Matter Of Caring

Terry J. Moody, Ph.D., DABPS, Child & Adolescent Psychologist
Diplomate, American Board of Psychological Specialties
Director, Child & Adolescent Services

THE MINIRTH CLINIC
Phone: 972/669-1733
Fax: 972/669-1403

2301 N. Greenville Ave., Ste. #200
Richardson, Texas 75082

THE MINIRTH CLINIC
A Matter Of Caring

SIHAM ZAKHARY
L.M.S.W., A.C.P., A.B.E.C.S.W., L.M.F.T., L.C.D.C., N.C.A.C.

THE MINIRTH CLINIC
Phone: 972/669-1733
Fax: 972/669-1403

2301 N. Greenville Ave., Ste. #200
Richardson, Texas 75082

THE MINIRTH CLINIC
A Matter Of Caring

TERI FUSILIER, M.A.B.C., L.P.C.

THE MINIRTH CLINIC
Phone: 972/669-1733
Fax: 972/669-1403

2301 N. Greenville Ave., Ste. #200
Richardson, Texas 75082

THE MINIRTH CLINIC
A Matter Of Caring

MINIRTH CLINIC, P.A.
Psychiatric and Counseling Center

THE MINIRTH CLINIC
Phone: 972/669-1733
Fax: 972/669-1403

2301 N. Greenville Avenue #200
Richardson, Texas 75082

THE MINIRTH CLINIC
A Matter Of Caring

FRANK B. MINIRTH, M.D.
Diplomate American Board of Psychiatry & Neurology

THE MINIRTH CLINIC
Phone: 972/669-1733
Fax: 972/669-1403

2301 N. Greenville Avenue #200
Richardson, Texas 75082

RESOURCE O

Genetic Factors in Psychiatric Disorders

Genetic Factors May Predispose to Psychological Problems

While we do not inherit psychological problems, it is possible to inherit a certain physical (genetic) makeup that may predispose us to certain psychological problems. A number of studies support this contention. These studies in no way nullify the spiritual dimension. We still make choices and are responsible for those choices. Here are some of the studies. Schizophrenia occurs in only 1 percent of the general population. However, if one parent is schizophrenic, the risk rises to 10 percent. If both parents are schizophrenic, the risk is 50 percent. If a fraternal, nonidentical twin becomes schizophrenic, there is a 10 percent chance that the other will also. By contrast, if an identical twin becomes schizophrenic, there is a 90 percent chance that the other will also if they have been raised together and around 80 percent if reared apart.

The occurrence of manic-depressive psychosis also provides evidence that there may be a physical predisposition to certain psychological problems. Close relatives of manic-depressives are twenty times more susceptible than the general population. Studies of twins (including twins reared apart) give nearly irrefutable evidence that there is a genetic factor. Most striking is genetic-linkage research indicating that in certain types of manic-depressive psychosis, the weakness is actually carried by the new X-chromosome in some cases and chromosome 11 or 18 in others.

Moreover, various studies have shown that there may be a genetic weakness involved in many other cases of depression. For example, 50 percent of the victims have a family history of depression. If a fraternal twin suffers from depression, there is only about a 10 percent chance that the other will too. However, if the twins are identical, the risk jumps to 76 percent. Even if they were reared apart, the risk runs as high as 67 percent.

Other disorders also point to a possible genetic factor. For example, 40 percent of individuals with OCD (obsessive-compulsive disorder) have a first-degree relative with OCD. Also, at least 35 percent of individuals with ADHD (attention deficit/hyperactivity disorder) have a first-degree relative with ADHD.

The research is perhaps the most interesting in the area of identical twins. Even the personality traits to some degree are inherited. Identical twins reared apart from birth show personality and behavioral similarities.

A . . . set of identical twins from Bouchard's University of Minnesota study of the roles of genetics vs. environment provides some striking support for the prominence of the genetic influence. Jim Springer and Jim Lewis were separated four weeks after their birth in 1940. They grew up forty-five miles apart in Ohio. After they were reunited in 1979, they discovered they had some eerie similarities: both chain-smoked Salems, both drove the same model blue Chevrolet, both chewed their fingernails, and both had dogs named Toy. Further, they had both vacationed in the same neighborhood in Florida. And when tested for such personality traits as sociability and self-control, they responded almost identically (Robert C. Carson, James N. Butcher, James C. Coleman, *Abnormal Psychology and Modern Life*, Eighth Edition, p. 57).

The data are overwhelming. While it would be wrong to conclude that mental disorders are inherited, a genetic weakness which predisposes to certain psychological conditions is inherited. That weakness may be manifested under stress. (The figure below summarizes research studies indicating that some psychological problems may be genetically related.)

Genetic Factors in Psychiatric Disorders

Genetic factors may make us vulnerable to certain mental problems. While, in general, people do not inherit mental problems, each of us inherits a certain biochemical and physiologic makeup. This makeup may predispose certain individuals, when they encounter stressful situations, to manifest symptoms (e.g., hallucinations, sleep disturbance) of various disorders. Research studies indicate that an inherited physical (genetic) weakness may make some families susceptible to specific psychological problems:

1. **Schizophrenia** occurs in only about 1 percent of the general population, but Kallman and Kety have discovered that the risk is much higher if a person has a close relative who has suffered from the disorder:
   a. One parent: 10 percent risk
   b. Both parents: 50 percent
   c. Sibling: 10 percent

d. Fraternal twin: 10 percent

e. Identical twin: 80 to 90 percent

2. **Manic-depressive psychosis** occurs in about .5 to 1 percent of the general population.

    a. A parent or sibling—10 percent. In 90 percent of the cases of bipolar psychosis, there is a first-degree relative with the disorder.

    b. Fraternal twin raised in the same home: 26 percent

    c. Identical twin raised in the same home: 66–96 percent

    d. Identical twin raised separately: 75 percent

3. **Depression** also seems to occur relatively often in certain families. In 30 percent of the cases of depression, there is a family history. As in other disorders, if one twin suffers, the risk to the other twin is high:

    a. Fraternal twin: 7–29 percent

    b. Identical twin raised in the same home: 60–76 percent

    c. Identical twin raised separately: 44–67 percent

4. **OCD (obsessive-compulsive disorder)** individuals will have a first-degree relative with OCD in 40 percent of the time.

5. **ADHD (attention deficit/hyperactivity disorder)** individuals will have a first-degree relative with ADHD 35 percent of the time.

Phone Numbers Frequently Used by Counselors

The Christian counselor often needs quick access to various phone numbers. Below are some common ones. I am not recommending any specific phone number or numbers.

Counseling Services

1-800-THERAPIST
America's Crisis Pregnancy Helpline: 1-800-672-2296
American Association of Christian Counselors: 1-800-526-8673
The Minirth Clinic, Dallas, Texas: 1-888-646-4784
Peacemakers: 1-406-256-1583

Discipleship Ministries

Campus Crusade for Christ: 1-800-989-7130
Fellowship of Christian Athletes: 1-800-289-0909
The Navigators: 1-719-598-1212
Young Life: 1-214-265-1505

Hospitals with Christian Programs

The Minirth Christian Program: 1-888-646-4784

Residential Placement

Hope Directory for Residential Placement Issues: 1-903-881-9090, Ext. 3003

Support Groups

ADHD

 ADHD Warehouse: 1-800-233-9273
 National Attention Deficit Disorder Association: 1-847-432-ADDA
 C.H.A.D.D.: 1-800-233-4050

AIDS

 AIDS Hotline: 1-800-342-2437

Alcoholism

 1-800-222-0469

Alzheimer's

 1-800-272-3900

Child Abuse/Issues

 Child Abuse Hotline: 1-800-422-4453
 National Domestic Violence Hotline: 1-800-799-SAFE
 National Runaway Switchboard: 1-800-621-4000

Drug Abuse and Other Addictive Behavior

 Focus on Recovery Helpline: 1-800-234-0420
                              1-800-234-0246
 National Council on Compulsive Gambling: 1-800-522-4700
 Substance Abuse Info—Treatment Referrals: 1-800-662-4357

Epilepsy

 Epilepsy Foundation of America: 1-800-332-1000

Learning Disabilities

 Learning Disabilities Association of America: 1-412-341-1515

OCD

 Obsessive Compulsive Anonymous: 1-516-739-0662

Suicide

    National Alliance for the Mentally Ill Helpline: 1-800-950-NAMI
                                                  1-800-633-3760
    American Association of Suicidology: 1-202-237-2280
                                                  1-800-SUICIDE

Veteran's Administration

    1-800-827-1000

Other Numbers

    Big Creek Ranch for Family Retreats: 1-888-646-4784
    Christian Marriage Enrichment/H. Norman Wright: 1-800-875-7560
    Focus on the Family Institute: 1-800-A-FAMILY
    National Association of Anorexia Nervosa and Associated Disorders: 1-847-831-3438
    National Depressive and Manic-Depressive Association: 1-800-82N-DMDA
    National Foundation for Depressive Illness: 1-800-248-4344
    National Institute of Mental Health: 1-301-496-3421

Physical Causes of Psychological Problems

The Complex Nature of Man

Man has a complex nature; that is, he is a physical, psychological, and spiritual creature, and all of these dimensions are interrelated. That man is a physical creature with physical weaknesses is obvious. It has been said that man begins to die at birth. After the age of forty, literally thousands of brain cells die daily. Man is constantly struggling against physical disease. What is not so obvious is that man's physical condition is integrally related to his psychological and spiritual condition. Man is a whole. What affects him physically affects him psychologically and spiritually as well. A physical disease can lead to psychological and/or spiritual problems—and vice versa. This section explores ways in which the various dimensions of the complex nature of man are interdependent.

Physical Problems Can Produce Emotional Problems

Man's physical condition has a direct bearing on his emotional health. For example, certain diseases, as well as certain drugs intended to relieve physical problems, can produce symptoms of depression. Among the diseases which can cause depression are viral illnesses (mononucleosis and pneumonia), endocrine disorders (hypothyroidism), cancer of the pancreas, and multiple sclerosis. Depression can also be an aftereffect of a variety of drugs, including major and minor tranquilizers, birth-control pills, diet pills, medication for high blood pressure, and alcohol.

Symptoms of anxiety are also often interconnected with man's physical condition. Tenseness, trembling, and even panic can be induced by endocrine disorders (hyperthyroidism), hormone abnormalities (hypoglycemia), tumors (phenochromocytoma), and various drugs (caffeine, marijuana, LSD, PCP, amphetamines).

Psychosis or a loss of touch with reality is another emotional disturbance that may be rooted in physical problems. Among the diseases that may result in psychosis are porphyria, Wilson's disease, Huntington's chorea, endocrine disorders (hyperthyroidism), and tumors of the temporal lobe of the brain. In addition, many drugs can cause one to lose contact with reality. They include illegal drugs (amphetamines, cocaine, LSD, PCP, and marijuana); prescriptions designed to combat seizures, depression, Parkinson's disease, or tuberculosis; alcohol; and even over-the-counter medications (nasal sprays, bromide-containing compounds to relieve anxiety, and sleeping pills).

It should also be mentioned that certain physical problems can produce changes in personality. Most notable in this connection is the problem of senility. (See below for an extensive list of physical conditions which can lead to emotional problems.)

---

*Physical Causes of Psychological Problems**

1. Physical causes of depression
   a. Viral illnesses: mononucleosis, pneumonia.
   b. Endocrine disorders: hypothyroidism, Cushing's syndrome, Addison's disease.
   c. Electrolyte abnormalities: hypermagnesemia.
   d. Other diseases: multiple sclerosis, cancer of the pancreas, dementia, rheumatoid arthritis.
   e. Endogenous depression (biochemical, genetically induced depression).
   f. "Masked depression" (this condition is characterized by physical complaints [such as headaches] which seem to have no organic pathology).
   g. Drugs: Both prescription drugs (Valium; medications for high blood pressure, birth control, psychosis) and illegal drugs (amphetamines).
   h. Alcohol.

2. Physical causes of anxiety
   a. Tumors: phenochromocytoma.
   b. Mitral-valve prolapse (this is the underlying problem in 30 to 40 percent of patients suffering from feelings of panic).
   c. Endocrine abnormalities: hyperthyroidism.
   d. Electrolyte abnormalities: hypomagnesemia, hypercalcemia (breast cancer).
   e. Hormone abnormalities: hypoglycemia (a temporary tense feeling and tremor follow the release of adrenaline).

*This list is not intended to be exhaustive.

    f.   Dementia (chronic organic brain syndrome) or delirium (acute organic brain syndrome).

    g.   Other diseases: vestibular disease, basilar-artery disease.

    h.   Hyperactivity.

    i.   Drugs: caffeine (more than 500 milligrams or 4 to 5 cups of coffee per day), prescription drugs (minor tranquilizers; medication for depression or psychosis can induce tremors), and illegal drugs (amphetamines, marijuana, LSD, and PCP can cause panic).

    j.   Alcohol (withdrawal, delirium tremens).

3. Physical causes of psychosis
    a.   Tumors, especially in the limbic system (psychosis occurs in 5 percent of the cases of temporal-lobe tumors).
    b.   Endocrine abnormalities: hypothyroidism, hyperthyroidism.
    c.   Other diseases: Huntington's chorea, porphyria, Wilson's disease.
    d.   Head trauma.
    e.   Drugs: prescription drugs (atropine, medication to combat seizures [Dilantin], depression, Parkinson's disease, tuberculosis, alcoholism [Antabuse]), over-the-counter drugs (nasal sprays, bromide-containing compounds to relieve anxiety, sleeping pills), and illegal drugs (amphetamines, cocaine, LSD, PCP, marijuana).
    f.   Alcohol: Krosakoff's psychosis.

4. Physical causes of personality changes (e.g., accentuation of basic characteristics or release of inhibitions)

    a.   Viral illnesses: Creutzfeldt-Jakob syndrome.
    b.   Temporal-lobe epilepsy.
    c.   Other diseases: multiple sclerosis, systemic lupus erythematosus.
    d.   Trauma ("punch drunk").
    e.   Senility.
    f.   Drugs: marijuana (amotivational syndrome), LSD, PCP.
    g.   Alcohol.

5. Physical causes of obsessive-compulsive disorder (repeated stereotyped behavior)
    a.   Temporal-lobe epilepsy.
    b.   Drugs: amphetamines.

6. Physical causes of apathy
   a. Tumor of the right hemisphere of the brain.
   b. Other diseases: Alzheimer's disease, Pick's disease, normal-pressure hydrocephalus.
   c. Trauma.
   d. Alcohol: Wernicke's syndrome.

7. Physical causes of violence
   a. Temporal-lobe epilepsy.
   b. Drugs: amphetamines, LSD, PCP.
   c. Alcohol.

8. Physical causes of abnormal religious preoccupation
   a. Temporal-lobe epilepsy.
   b. Manic-depressive psychosis.
   c. Drugs.

9. Physical causes of amnesia
   a. Cardiovascular accident.
   b. Trauma.
   c. Alcohol.

10. Physical causes of insomnia.
    a. Sleep apnea.
    b. Myoclonic jerks.
    c. Various medical diseases.
    d. Drugs: caffeine, amphetamines.

11. Physical cause of hyperactivity (impulsiveness, distractibility, lack of concentration, poor school performance, behavior problems)—underdevelopment of the nervous system.

12. Physical causes of confusion
    a. Degenerative diseases: Alzheimer's disease, Pick's disease.
    b. Vascular-circulatory disorders with relative ischemia: arrhythmias, congestive heart failure, repeated emboli and infarcts.
    c. Viral infections: encephalitis, chronic meningitis, herpes, influenza, measles, mumps.
    d. Chronic metabolic encephalopathy: endocrine abnormalities (hypoglycemia), circulatory disturbances (hypoxia).
    e. Tumors.
    f. Dementia or delirium.

g.   Other diseases: multiple sclerosis, normal-pressure hydrocephalus, septicemia, viremia, Parkinson's disease.

h.   Trauma: concussion, subdural hemorrhage.

i.   Nutritional deficiencies: lack of thiamin, niacin, vitamin B_{12}.

j.   Drugs: steroids, bromides, barbiturates, lithium, opiates, antibiotics, anticholinergics including over-the-counter sleep medications.

k.   Alcohol.

l.   Mental retardation (in this case apparent confusion is actually inability to understand).

Psychiatric Medications

A List of Psychiatric Medications by Categories of Use

Regardless of one's view of psychiatric medications today, the Christian counselor needs to be aware of common names he or she will hear from their clients. The following is a list by category of usage of psychiatric medications. Some are used on-label; others are used off-label such as some of the anticonvulsants that are used for pain relief and mood stabilization.

Categories of Psychiatric Medications

1. **Antidepressants**
    A. Serotonin-Specific Reuptake Inhibitors
        Citalopram (Celexa)
        Escitalopram (Lexapro)
        Fluoxetine (Prozac, Sarafem)
        Fluvoxamine (LuVox)
        Paroxetine (Paxil)
        Sertraline (Zoloft)
    B. Tertiary Amine Tricyclic Antidepressants
        Amitriptyline (Elavil, Endep)
        Clomipramine (Anafranil)
        Doxepin (Adapin, Sinequan)
        Imipramine (Tofranil)
        Trimipramine (Surmontil)
    C. Secondary Amine Tricyclic Antidepressants

      Desipramine (Norpramin)
      Nortriptyline (Pamelor, Aventyl)
      Protriptyline (Vivactil)
  D. Tetracyclic Antidepressants
      Amoxapine (Asendin)
      Maprotiline (Ludiomil)
      Mirtazapine (Remeron)
  E. Monoamine Oxidase Inhibitors
      Phenelzine (Nardil)
      Tranylcypromine (Parnate)
  F. Atypical Antidepressants
      Bupropion (Wellbutrin and Wellbutrin SR)
      Duloxatine (Symbalta)
      Nefazodone (Serzone)
      Trazodone (Desyrel)
      Venlafaxine (Effexor and Effexor XR)

2. **Antipsychotics**
  A. High-Potency Antipsychotics
      Fluphenazine (Prolixin)
      Haloperidol (Haldol)
      Pimozide (Orap)
      Thiothixene (Navane)
      Trifluoperazine (Stelazine)
  B. Mid-Potency Antipsychotics
      Loxapine (Loxitane)
      Molindone (Moban)
      Perphenazine (Triafon)
  C. Low-Potency Antipsychotics
      Chlorpromazine (Thorazine)
      Mesoridazine (Serentil)
      Thioridazine (Mellaril)
  D. Atypical Antipsychotics
      Aripiprazole (Abilify)
      Clozapine (Clozaril)
      Olanzapine (Zyprexa, Zydis)
      Quetiapine (Seroquel)
      Risperidone (Risperdal)
      Ziprasidone (Geodon)

3. **Anxiolytics (Antianxiety Agents)**
  A. Anxiolytic Benzodiazepines

Alprazolam (Xanax)
Chlordiazepoxide (Librium, Libritabs)
Clonazepam (Klonopin)
Clorazepate (Tranxene)
Diazepam (Valium)
Halazepam (Paxipam)
Lorazepam (Ativan)
Oxazepam (Serax)
B. Non-Benzodiazepine Anxiolytics
Buspirone (BuSpar)
Hydroxyzine (Atarax, Vistaril)
C. Benzodiazepine Hypnotics (Medications for Insomnia)
Flurazepam (Dalmane)
Estazolam (ProSom)
Quazepam (Doral)
Temazepam (Restoril)
Triazolam (Halcion)
D. Non-Benzodiazepine Hypnotics (Medications for Insomnia)
Chloral Hydrate (Somnote)
Diphenhydramine (Benadryl)
Zaleplon (Sonata)
Zolpidem (Ambien)
E. Barbiturates
Amobarbital (Amytal)
Pentobarbital (Nembutal)

4. **Mood Stabilizers**
A. Lithium Carbonate (Eskalith, Lithonate, Eskalith CR)
B. Anticonvulsants
Carbamazepine (Tegretol)
Gabapentin (Neurontin)
Levetiracetam (Keppra)
Oxcarbazepine (Trileptal)
Topiramate (Topamax)
Zonisamide (Zonagran)
C. Benzodiazepines
Alprazolam (Xanax)
Clonazepam (Klonopin)
Lorazepam (Ativan)
D. Calcium Channel Inhibitors
Amlodipine (Norvasc)

Isradipine (DynaCirc)
Nicardipine (Cardene)
Nifedipine (Procardia)
Nimodipine (Nimoptop)
Nisoldipine (Sular)
Verapamil (Calan)

5. **Attention-Deficit/Hyperactivity Disorder (ADHD)**

A. Psychostimulants
    Dextroamphetamine + Amphetamine (Adderall)
    Dexstroamphetamine (Dexedrine)
    Methylphenidate (Concerta, Focalin, Metadate, Methylin, Ritalin)
    Pemoline (Cylert)

B. Atomoxetine (Strattera)

C. Alpha Agonists
    Clonidine (Catapress)
    Guanfacine (Tenex)

D. Antidepressants
    Bupropin (Wellbutrin)
    Venlafaxine (Effexor)

E. Narcolepsy Medication
    Modafinil (Provigil)

6. **Substance Dependence**

Management of Substance Dependence
    Bupropion (Zyban)
    Clonidine (Catapres, Catapres-TTS)
    Disulfiram (Antabuse)
    Methadone (Dolophine)
    Naltrexone (ReVia)

7. **Dementia (Alzheimer's Type)**

Donepezil (Aricept)
Galanfamine (Reminyl)
Rivastigmine (Exelon)
Tacrine (Cognex)

8. **Medications for Pain**

A. Medications for Acute Migraine Headache Pain
    Almotriptan (Axert)
    Butalbitol, Acetaminophen, Caffeine Combination (Esgic)
    Butorphanol Nasal Spray (Stadol)
    Dihydruergotamine Mesylate Nasal Spray (Migranal)
    Ergotamine (Wygesic)

Frovatriptan (Frova)
Isomethopetene (Midrin)
Naratriptan (Amerge)
Rizatriptan (Maxalt)
Sumatriptan (Imitrex)
Sumatriptan Nasal Spray (Imitrex)
Zolmitriptan (Zomig)

B. Medications for the Prophylactic Treatment of Migraine

Acetylsalicylic Acid (Aspirin)
Amitriptyline (Elavil)
Clonidine (Catapress)
Cyproheptadine (Periactin)
Ergonovine (Maleate)
Fluoxetine (Prozac)
Imipramine (Tofranil)
Methysergide (Sansert)
Propranolol (Inderol)
Sertraline (Zoloft)
Verapamil (Calan)

C. Nonsterioidal Anti-Inflammatory Pain Medications

Acetaminophen (Tylenol, Datril)
Acetylsalicylic Acid (Aspirin)
Celecoxib (Celebrex)
Choline Magnesium Salicylate (Trilisate)
Choline Salicylate (Anthropan)
Diclofenac (Voltaren, Cataflam)
Diclofenac Sustained Release (Voltaren-XR)
Diflunisal (Dolobid)
Etodolac (Lodine)
Fenopprofen Calcium (Nalfon)
Flurbiprofen (Ansaid)
Ibuprofen (Motrin, Advil, Rufen)
Indomethacin (Indocin, Indometh)
Ketoprofen (Orudis, Oruvail)
Ketorolac Tromethamine (Toradol)
Magnesium Salicylate
Meclofenamate Sodium (Meclomen)
Mefenamic Acid (Ponstel)
Nabumetone (Relafen)
Naproxen (Naprosyn, Anaprox, Aleve [OTC])

Oxaprozin (Daypro)
Piroxicam (Feldene)
Rofecoxib (Vioxx)
Sodium Salicylate
Sulindac (Clinoril)
Tolmetin (Tolectin)
Valdecoxib (Bextra)
D. Opioid Pain Medications
Codeine
Hydrocodone (in Lorcet, Lortab, Vicodin)
Hydromorphone (Dilaudid)
Levorphanol (Levo-Dromoran)
Meperidine (Demerol)
Methadone (Dolophine)
Morphine
Morphine Controlled Release (MS Contin, Roxanol, Oramorph)
Oxycodone (Roxicodone, Percocet, Percodan, Tylox)
Oxymorphone (Numorphan)
Tramadol (Ultram)
E. Neuropatic Pain Medications
Tricyclic Antidepressants
Amitriptyline (Elavil)
Desipramine (Norpramin)
Nortriptyline (Norpramin)
Nontricylic Antidepressants
Sustained-Release Bupropion (Wellbutrin SR)
Anticonvulsants
Carbamazepine (Tegretol)
Clonazepam (Klonopin)
Gabapentin (Neurontin)
Levetiracetam (Keppra)
Oxycabazepine (Trileptal)
Topiramate (Topamax)
Zonisamide (Zonegran)
9. **Antiparkinsonian Drugs**
A. Dopamine Precursors
Carbidopa (Lodosyn)
Levadopa (Larodopa)
Levadopa-carbidopa (Sinemet)
B. Dopamine Agonists

     Bromocriptine (Parlodel)

     Pergalide (Permax)

     Pramipexole (Mirapex)

     Ropinirole (Requip)

C. Entacapone (Comtan)

D. Anticholinergic Medications

     Benztropine (Cogentin)

     Biperiden (Akineton)

     Ethopropazine (Parsidol)

     Orphenadrine (Norflex)

     Procyclidine (Kemadrin)

     Trihexyphenidyl (Artane)

E. Amantadine (Symmetrel)

F. MAO-B Inhibitor

     Selegiline (Eldepry)

G. Antihistamine Medication

     Diphenhydramine (Benadryl)

10. Anorexiants (Weight-Loss Medication)

A. Fat Blocker

     Orlistat (Xenical)

B. Serotonin, Norepinephrine Reuptake Inhibitor: Sibutramine (Merida)

C. Sympathomimetics

     Amphetamine (Biphetamine)

     Benzephetamine (Didrex)

     Diethylpropion (Tenuate)

     Mazindol (Mazanor, Sanorex)

     Methamphetamine (Desoxyn)

     Phendimetrazine (Adipost, Bontril)

     Phenmetrazine (Preludin)

     Phentermine (Adipex, Fastin, Ionamin)

An Overview of Secular Psychotherapies from a Christian Perspective

The Christian counselor is often asked his opinion on various secular psychotherapies. Here is an outline summary from a Christian perspective.

It has been estimated that more than 250 methods of psychotherapy are in use today. How is the novice counselor to know which one is best? From our experience as Christian psychiatrists, we have come to the conclusion that the wisest policy is to follow what we have chosen to designate the "Christian eclectic approach." Central to this approach is our conviction that the Bible must be the foundation of every therapeutic effort. The Bible is divine revelation. No scientific knowledge can produce results equal to those produced by the Word of God.

On the other hand, natural revelation from scientific data such as the discovery of penicillin in the 1920s can be helpful. With this in mind one may legitimately draw from the methodologies of various schools. It would be naïve to think that one school has discovered most of the truth while the others have little. Many schools have a measure of the truth, but none has all of it. Therefore, it is necessary to be selective. It would be foolish to expect all counselees to respond to one therapeutic method. Rather, the counselor should have a variety of methods at his disposal and use the one that will best help the counselee. In other words, it is the counselor, not the counselee, who should adapt. In choosing the most appropriate method or combination of methods to fit the particular situation, the wise counselor will always be mindful that the only absolute standard is the Word of God.

With the proliferation of various schools of thought, it will be helpful to place them in several broad categories. This grouping will give some sense of order to the Christian counselor who is groping amid the confusing complexity of methods available today. Of all the attempts to categorize the various schools of psychotherapy, that of Toksoz Karaus is most useful for our purposes. We will summarize his classification of schools into three basic divisions: insight oriented, behavior oriented, and experiential oriented. We will then touch briefly on a fourth (the biochemical oriented) and add our own (the Christian eclectic approach).

Insight-Oriented Schools

The insight-oriented schools teach that mental problems develop because of unconscious, unresolved conflicts from childhood. Mental health results as a person begins to gain in-depth insight into how these unconscious conflicts affect him today. The ultimate goal is to help the counselee resolve these conflicts. An example of the insight-oriented schools is psychoanalysis (including all its short-term variations). (See figure below for lists of representative techniques used by the insight-oriented schools and by the other major schools of secular psychotherapy.)

Behavior-Oriented Schools

The behavior-oriented schools teach that mental problems manifest themselves in inappropriate behavior. This inappropriate behavior may have been learned or conditioned at an early age; it may involve overt fears or faulty beliefs. In any event, it is the view of the behavior-oriented schools that new behavior can be learned. Desensitization techniques are used in behavior modification; new beliefs are instilled by cognitive therapy; more responsible behavior is taught in reality therapy.

Techniques of the Major Schools of Secular Psychotherapy

1. **Insight-Oriented Therapy**
   a. Free association
   b. Confrontation of resistances
   c. Clarification of issues
   d. Interpretation of feelings
   e. "Working through" areas of conflict
   f. Transference
   g. Corrective emotional experience

2. **Behavior-Oriented Therapy**
   a. Modeling
   b. Role playing
   c. Behavior rehearsal
   d. Assertiveness training
   e. Positive reinforcement
   f. Offering advice or suggestions

g. Problem solving
h. Goal setting
i. Building better support systems (family, community organizations)
j. Challenging false beliefs (e.g., arbitrary inferences, overgeneralizations)
k. Offering alternatives to false beliefs
l. Assigning tasks to the counselee and grading his performance

3. **Experiential-Oriented Therapy**
   a. Catharsis
   b. Self-actualization
   c. Listening
   d. Reflection
   e. Unconditional acceptance of the counselee

4. **Biochemical-Oriented Therapy**
   a. Major tranquilizers for psychosis
   b. SSRIs, atypical antidepressants, tricyclics, tetracyclics, or monoamine oxidase inhibitors for depression
   c. Minor tranquilizers for anxiety
   d. Lithium for manic symptoms

Experiential-Oriented Schools

In general, the experiential-oriented schools focus on feelings. Their techniques often revolve around getting the client in touch with his true feelings or arousing negative feelings. Examples of experiential-oriented schools include the Rogerian school, the gestalt school, and primal-scream therapy.

The wise counselor draws from each of the three groups we have briefly characterized. In some instances one of these approaches is obviously the best course to follow. But it is often advisable to make use of all of them. Take, for example, the particular program we adopted in treating a young woman who came to our office for counseling. (1) She was helped to gain *insight* into the unresolved conflicts she had with her father and into the negative effects these conflicts had on her relationship with her husband. (2) She was also helped to deal with bitter *feelings* which had been there all along but had been repressed and manifested themselves in passive-aggressive behavior. (3) She was encouraged to make appropriate changes in her daily *behavior* in order to improve relationships with her husband and friends.

Biochemical-Oriented Schools

We must also mention the biochemical-oriented schools, which may have many followers and may in fact be the major force in psychiatry today. The proponents of these schools teach that mental problems are the results of biochemical, physiological, and neurological abnormalities. In their view mental problems can be resolved by correcting these biochemical abnormalities.

The Christian Eclectic Approach

Finally we consider the category of "Christian counseling" (see John D. Carter, "Secular and Sacred Models of Psychology and Religion," *Journal of Psychology and Theology*, 1977, 197–98). There are various subdivisions within this category: (1) those schools which place greater emphasis on psychology than on Scripture; (2) those schools which feel that Scripture and psychology parallel each other but never meet; (3) those schools which feel that Scripture is opposed to psychology; and (4) those schools which integrate the two. We place ourselves firmly within the last subdivision. Of course, even here it must be emphasized that Scripture is divine revelation and can produce supernatural results. Psychology in and of itself can never do what Scripture can. Psychology can be extremely helpful. One can learn much from it. But formal psychological theory and Scripture are not on the same plane. (See "Four Types of Therapy" chart below for a comparison of the Christian approach with the insight-oriented, behavior-oriented, and experiential-oriented schools).

Now that we have briefly looked at the four major groups of secular psychotherapy and those schools which are categorized as "Christian counseling," it is time to restate our approach. We incorporate in our counseling the methods employed by all four major groups mentioned previously. We examine each case on an individual basis and carefully determine which of the methods will be of greatest use. We take the best from each of the major categories of psychotherapy. We employ, then, an eclectic approach. But underlying all our decisions in these matters is a burning concern to ensure that the Bible is central to our counseling techniques. Not only is the Word of God to be used in conjunction with the therapies of the secular schools, it is to be the overriding factor. Thus, it is that we choose to label our counseling method the "Christian eclectic approach."

General Limitations of Secular Psychology

1. Illogical that one approach cures all.
2. Avoid future (focus on past or present).
3. Scientific research—therapist (warmth, genuine, empathizing), not the therapy.
4. Counselor should flex, not counselee.
5. Schools not original—often restatement of biblical facts.

Counseling Techniques from the Bible

1. Advice   Proverbs 19:20
2. Encouragement   2 Corinthians 1:3–4
3. Support   Romans 1:11–12
4. Education   Letters of Paul
5. Confession   James 5:16
6. Positive verbal reinforcement   Romans 1:8
7. Modeling—Christ and the disciples, Paul and Timothy

Four Types of Therapy*

	Insight Oriented	Behavior Oriented	Experiential Oriented	Christian
Representative Schools	1. Psychoanalysis (Freud) 2. Analytical psychology (Jung) 3. Individual psychology (Adler) 4. Psychoanalytic psychotherapy (Fromm, Reichmann) 5. Short-term psychotherapy (Sifneos, Malan) 6. Hypnoanalysis (Wolberg) 7. Brief or emergency psychotherpy	1. Reciprocal inhibition or behavior therapy (Wolpe) 2. Modeling therapy (Bandura) 3. Directive psychology (Thorne) 4. Behavior modification (for use with inpatients) 5. Rational-emotive therapy (Ellis) 6. Reality therapy (Glasser) 7. Transactional analysis (Berne) 8. Biofeedback (Green)	1. Client-centered (Rogers) 2. Gestalt (Peris) 3. Primal scream (Janov) 4. Logotherapy (Frankl) 5. Reparenting	1. Scripture integrated with but regarded as more important than psychology
Basic Divisions	A continuum from short-term to psychoanalysis	1. Earlier schools, emphasis on overt fears and behavior 2. More recent schools, emphasis on beliefs (Ellis) 3. Majority of most-recent schools, emphasis on biofeedback	1. Philosophic (Rogers) 2. Somatic	
Mental Disorders Treated	Neuroses, personality disorders	Some neuroses, psychoses	Low self-image	
Concept of Pathology	Unconscious conflicts	Inappropriate learned behavior	Loss of human potential	
Goal of Treatment	Conflict resolution	Removal of inappropriate behavior	Actualization of potential	

Four Types of Therapy*

	Insight Oriented	Behavior Oriented	Experiential Oriented	Christian
Mode of Attaining Goal	In-depth insight	Direct learning	Immediate experiencing	Eclectic approach, depending on needs of the individual
Time Focus	Past	Objective present	The moment	Past, present, future
Type of Treatment	Long-term, intense	Short-term, not intense	Short-term, intense	Length and intensity vary
Counselor's Task	To comprehend unconscious	To shape behavior	To express himself openly	To understand and treat the problems of the whole person
Counselor's Role	Indirect, to reflect and interrupt	Direct and practical, to advise	To accept the counselee without condition	To determine and utilize an approach suitable to the particular situation (see 1 Thess. 5:14)
Techniques	Free association, transference	Conditioning	A variety including verbal and somatic methods	Use of Scripture and scientific methods
Treatment Model	Doctor-patient (therapeutic alliance)	Teacher-student (learning alliance)	Peer-peer (human alliance)	Shepherd-member of flock (spiritual alliance)
Nature of Relationship	Artificial relationship for the purpose of finding a cure	Genuine, but for the sake of finding a cure	Genuine, but primarily to find a cure	Genuine relationship which is used in the search for a cure
Crucial Point Ignored by the General Theory	Insight alone may not result in change	Man is more than a computer	Man is not all good	

*Most of this chart is based on Toksaz B. Karaus, "Psychotherapies: An Overview," *American Journal of Psychiatry* 134.8 (1977): 851–63. Used by permission of the American Psychiatric Association. The characterization of Christian counseling is based in part on John D. Carter, "Secular and Sacred Models of Psychology and Religion," *Journal of Psychology and Theology* (1977): 197–208, and in part on our own ideas and experience.

Limitations of the Secular Schools of Psychotherapy

A. General
B. Spiritual
    1. No standard of authority
    2. Willpower can be sufficient (Rom. 7:18)
    3. Man is basically selfish (Jer. 17:9)
    4. Limited to the psychological (1 Cor. 2:14)

RESOURCE T

Self-Rating Reports of Symptoms

Often the counselor needs to know which direction to head first. Also, the direction may change from visit to visit. What are the major concerns of the counselee? These forms, filled out by the counselee, may point to the right direction.

The following descriptions are taken from the DSM-IV. The DSM-IV is the official manual of mental disorders. It is not based on causes or cures but rather strictly on symptom criteria. Thus, it has broad acceptance. The format of "past, present, severity," etc. is my own. These are merely forms that may indicate a trend. They do not substitute for clinical judgment.

At the top of each evaluation is a scale of 0 to 10. If you check a significant amount of the symptoms on any form, then grade each of the criteria on a scale of 0 to 10.

0 = The symptom is not significant most of the time.

1 = The symptom is present most of the time to a small degree.

10 = The symptom is present most of the time to an extreme degree.

Name _____ Date _____

Self-Rating Report of Symptoms: An Overview

0————————————1————————————————————10

| Not significant most of the time. | Present a small amount most of the time to a significant degree. | As severe as possible. |

Please circle the numbers of your three most serious issues below.

1. Depression _____ Blue, sad, down feeling

2. Anxiety _____ Nervous, tense, apprehensive

3. Insomnia _____ Difficulty falling and staying asleep

4. Low energy _____ Tired

5. Anger _____ Irritability, anger

6. Low motivation _____ Low interests

7. Manic _____ Overly high, energetic, grandiose

8. Inattention _____ Trouble paying attention, distractible, forgetful

9. Behavior problems _____ (Specify) _____

10. Hyperactivity _____ Hyperactive, fidget, squirm

11. OCD _____ Repetitive, irrational worry or actions

12. Trouble functioning _____ At work, socially

13. Dysthymia _____ Sad mood most days for last two years

14. Stressor severity _____ (Specify) _____
   (Severity of current stressors, changes & events)

   _____ (A) Relationship stressors

   _____ (B) Finance stressors

   _____ (C) Job stressors

15. Confusion _____ (Specify) _____
   (Hearing voices, paranoid, trouble thinking logically, rambling speech, etc.)

16. Worry   _____

17. Pain   _____   (Specify) _____

18. Social fears   _____   Fears of social events

19. Eating issues _____   (A) Eating too much

                   _____   (B) Overconcern with perfection in weight

20. Guilt   _____

Your major concern today that you want addressed? _____
                                                  (Symptoms, side effects, behavioral problems, etc.)

Overall since your last visit, do you feel: (Please check one if applicable) ___ Improved

___ Same ___ Worse

Name _____ Date _____

Self-Rating Report of ADHD
(Attention-Deficit/Hyperactivity Disorder) Symptoms

0———————————1—————————————————10

| Not significant most of the time. | Present a small amount most of the time to a significant degree. | As severe as possible. |

Past   Present Severity 0–10

A. Either (1) or (2):

1. Six (or more) of the following symptoms of **inattention** have persisted for at least six months to a degree that is maladaptive and inconsistent with developmental level:

Inattention

____   ____   ____ a. Often fails to give close attention to details or makes careless mistakes in schoolwork, work, or other activities.

____   ____   ____ b. Often has difficulty sustaining attention in tasks or play activities.

____   ____   ____ c. Often does not seem to listen when spoken to directly.

____   ____   ____ d. Often does not follow through on instructions and fails to finish schoolwork, chores, or duties in the workplace (not due to oppositional behavior or failure to understand instructions).

____   ____   ____ e. Often has difficulty organizing tasks and activities.

____   ____   ____ f. Often avoids, dislikes, or is reluctant to engage in tasks that require sustained mental effort (such as schoolwork or homework).

____   ____   ____ g. Often loses things necessary for tasks or activities (e.g., toys, school assignments, pencils, books, or tools).

____   ____   ____ h. Is often easily distracted by extraneous stimuli.

____   ____   ____ i. Is often forgetful in daily activities.

2. Six (or more) of the following symptoms of **hyperactivity-impulsivity** have persisted for at least six months to a degree that is maladaptive and inconsistent with developmental level:

Hyperactivity

____ ____ ____   a. Often fidgets with hands or feet or squirms in seat.

____ ____ ____   b. Often leaves seat in classroom or in other situations in which remaining seated is expected.

____ ____ ____   c. Often runs about or climbs excessively in situations in which it is inappropriate (in adolescents or adults, may be limited to subjective feelings of restlessness).

____ ____ ____   d. Often has difficulty playing or engaging in leisure activities quietly.

____ ____ ____   e. Is often "on the go" or often acts as if "driven by a motor."

____ ____ ____   f. Often talks excessively.

Impulsivity

____ ____ ____   g. Often blurts out answers before questions have been completed.

____ ____ ____   h. Often has difficulty awaiting turn.

____ ____ ____   i. Often interrupts or intrudes on others (e.g., butts into conversations or games).

B. Some hyperactive-impulsive or inattentive symptoms that caused impairment were present before age seven years. Indicate please: _____

C. Some impairment from the symptoms is present in two or more settings (e.g., at school [or work] and at home). Indicate please: _____

D. There must be clear evidence of clinically significant impairment in social, academic, or occupational functioning. Indicate please: _____

Name _____ Date _____

Self-Rating or Family Rating Report of Dementia Symptoms

0————————————1————————————————————————10

| Not significant most of the time. | Present a small amount most of the time to a significant degree. | As severe as possible. |

Past   Present Severity 0–10

A. The development of multiple cognitive deficits manifested by both:

____   ____   ____   1. Memory impairment (impaired ability to learn new information or to recall previously learned information)

2. One (or more) of the following cognitive disturbances:

____   ____   ____   a. aphasia (language disturbance).
____   ____   ____   b. apraxia (impaired ability to carry out motor activities despite intact motor function).
____   ____   ____   c. agnosia (failure to recognize or identify objects despite intact sensory function).
____   ____   ____   d. disturbance in executive functioning (i.e., planning, organizing, sequencing, abstracting).

____   ____   ____   B. The cognitive deficits in Criteria A1 and A2 each cause significant impairment in social or occupational functioning and represent a significant decline from a previous level of functioning.

____   ____   ____   C. The course is characterized by gradual onset and continuing cognitive decline.

Name _____ Date _____

Self-Rating Report of Dopamine-like (Possible Psychotic-like) Symptoms

0————————1————————————————10

| Not significant most of the time. | Present a small amount most of the time to a significant degree. | As severe as possible. |

Past   Present Severity 0–10

A. I have the following "A" words.
1. Few words (alogia)
2. Low interests (apathy)
3. Lack of facial expression (affect flattening)
4. Lack of enjoyment of life (anhedonia)
5. In my own world in my brain (autistic)
6. Strongly see both sides of many opposite issues (ambivalent)

B. People tell me I have somewhat disorganized speech at times (loose associations).

C. I have at times:
1. Seen things that others do not.
2. Felt things that others do not.
3. Smelled things that others do not.
4. Heard voices that others do not.

D. I have felt that others:
1. Are watching me.
2. Are conspiring against me.
3. Are reading my mind.
4. Are inserting thoughts into my mind.
5. Would persecute me.

E. None of the above apply to me.

Name _____ Date _____

Self-Rating Report of Dysthymic Symptoms

0————————————1——————————————————————10

| Not significant most of the time. | Present a small amount most of the time to a significant degree. | As severe as possible. |

Past   Present   Severity 0–10

____   ____   ____   A. Depressed mood for most of the day, for more days than not, as indicated either by subjective account or observation by others, **for at least two years**. NOTE: In children and adolescents, mood can be irritable and duration must be at least one year.

B. Presence, while depressed, of two or more of the following:

____   ____   ____   1. Poor appetite or overeating.

____   ____   ____   2. Insomnia (not sleeping) or hypersomnia (sleeping too much).

____   ____   ____   3. Low energy or fatigue.

____   ____   ____   4. Low self-worth.

____   ____   ____   5. Poor concentration or difficulty making decisions.

____   ____   ____   6. Strongly see both sides of many opposite issues (Ambivalent)

____   ____   ____   C. The symptoms cause clinically significant distress or impairment in social, occupational, or other important areas of functioning.

Name _____ Date _____

Self-Rating Report of Generalized Anxiety Symptoms

0————————————1———————————————————————10
Not significant   Present a small amount   As severe as
most of the time.   most of the time to a   possible.
                         significant degree.

Past   Present Severity 0–10

____ ____ ____   A. Excessive anxiety and worry (apprehensive expectation), **occurring more days than not** for at least six months, about a number of events or activities (such as work or school performance).

____ ____ ____   B. The person finds it difficult to control worry.

                   C. The anxiety and worry are associated with three (or more) of the following six symptoms (with at least some symptoms present **for more days than not** for the past six months).
____ ____ ____   1. Restlessness or feeling keyed up or on edge.
____ ____ ____   2. Being easily fatigued.
____ ____ ____   3. Difficulty concentrating or mind going blank.
____ ____ ____   4. Irritability.
____ ____ ____   5. Muscle tension.
____ ____ ____   6. Sleep disturbance (difficulty falling or staying asleep, or restless unsatisfying sleep).

____ ____ ____   D. The focus of the anxiety is not confined to anxiety or worry concerning: being embarrassed in public, being contaminated, being away from home or close relatives, gaining weight, having multiple physical complaints, or having a serious illness, and the anxiety and worry do not occur exclusively from a past traumatic event.

____ ____ ____   E. The anxiety, worry, or physical symptoms cause significant distress or impairment in social, occupational, or other important areas of functioning.

Name _____ Date _____

Self-Rating Report of Hypomanic Symptoms

0———————————1——————————————————10

| Not significant most of the time. | Present a small amount most of the time to a significant degree. | As severe as possible. |

Past   Present   Severity 0–10

____   ____   ____   A. A distinct period of persistently elevated (increased), expansive (broad, both highs and lows), or irritable mood, lasting throughout at least four days, that is clearly different from the usual nondepressed mood.

B. During the period of mood disturbance, three (or more) of the following symptoms have persisted (four if the mood is only irritable) and have been present to a significant degree:

____   ____   ____   1. Inflated self-esteem or grandiosity (boasting, imposing, showy).

____   ____   ____   2. Decreased need for sleep (e.g., feels rested after only three hours of sleep).

____   ____   ____   3. More talkative than usual or pressure to keep talking.

____   ____   ____   4. Flight of ideas or subjective experience (self-understanding) that one's thoughts are racing.

____   ____   ____   5. Distractibility (i.e., attention too easily drawn to unimportant or irrelevant external stimuli).

____   ____   ____   6. Increase in goal-directed activity (either socially, at work or school, or sexually) or psychomotor agitation (anxiety that may result in hand wringing, pacing, or an inability to sit still).

____   ____   ____   7. Excessive involvement in pleasurable activities that have a high potential for painful consequences (e.g., engaging in unrestrained buying sprees, sexual indiscretions, or foolish business investments).

____   ____   ____   C. The episode is associated with an unequivocal change in functioning that is uncharacteristic of the person when not symptomatic.

____   ____   ____   D. The disturbance in mood and the change in functioning are observable by others.

Name _____ Date _____

Self-Rating Report of Major Depressive Symptoms

0——————————1———————————————————10

Not significant   Present a small amount   As severe as

most of the time.   most of the time to a   possible.

                      significant degree.

Past   Present Severity 0–10

A. Five or more of the following symptoms have been present during the same two-week period and represent a change from previous functioning; at least one of the symptoms is either (1) depressed mood or (2) loss of interest or pleasure.

____   ____   ____   1. Depressed mood most of the day, nearly every day, as indicated by either subjective report (e.g., feels sad or empty) or observation made by others (e.g., appears fearful). NOTE: In children and adolescents, can be irritable mood.

____   ____   ____   2. Markedly diminished interest or pleasure in all, or almost all, activities most of the day, nearly every day (as indicated by either subjective account or observation made by others).

____   ____   ____   3. Significant weight loss when not dieting or weight gain (e.g., a change of more than 5 percent of body weight in a month), or decrease or increase in appetite nearly every day. NOTE: In children, consider failure to make expected weight gains.

____   ____   ____   4. Insomnia (cannot sleep) or hypersomnia (sleeps too much) nearly every day.

____   ____   ____   5. Psychomotor (relating to muscle movement, combination of motor events, including disturbances) agitation or retardation nearly every day (observable by others, not merely subjective feelings of restlessness or being slowed down).

____   ____   ____   6. Fatigue or loss of energy nearly every day.

____   ____   ____   7. Feelings of worthlessness or excessive or inappropriate guilt (which may be delusional) nearly every day (not merely self-reproach or guilt about being sick).

____   ____   ____   8. Diminished ability to think, or concentrate, or increased indecisiveness, nearly every day (either by subjective account or as observed by others).

____   ____   ____   9. Recurrent thoughts of death (not just fear of dying), recurrent suicidal ideation without a specific plan, or a suicide attempt or a specific plan for committing suicide.

____   ____   ____   B. The symptoms cause clinically significant distress or impairment in social, occupational, or other important areas of functioning.

Name _____ Date _____

Self-Rating Report of Obsessive-Compulsive Symptoms

0————————————1————————————————————————10

Not significant　　　　Present a small amount　　　　　　　　As severe as
most of the time.　　　most of the time to a　　　　　　　　possible.
　　　　　　　　　　　significant degree.

Past　Present Severity 0–10

　　　　　　　　　　　A. Either obsessions or compulsions:

　　　　　　　　　　　Obsessions as defined by 1, 2, 3, and 4:
____　____　____　　1. Recurrent and persistent thoughts, impulses, or images that are experienced, at some time during the disturbance, as intrusive and inappropriate and that cause marked anxiety or distress.
____　____　____　　2. The thoughts, impulses, or images are not simply excessive worries about real-life problems.
____　____　____　　3. The person attempts to ignore or suppress such thoughts, impulses, or images, or to neutralize them with some other thought or action.
____　____　____　　4. The person recognizes that the obsessional thoughts, impulses, or images are a product of his or her own mind (not imposed from without as in thought insertion).

　　　　　　　　　　　Compulsions as defined by 1 and 2:
____　____　____　　1. Repetitive behaviors (e.g., hand washing, ordering, checking) or mental acts (e.g., praying, counting, repeating words silently) that the person feels driven to perform in response to an obsession, or according to rules that must be applied rigidly.
____　____　____　　2. The behaviors or mental acts are aimed at preventing or reducing distress or preventing some dreaded event or situation; however, these behaviors or mental acts either are not connected in a realistic way with what they are designed to neutralize or prevent or are clearly excessive.

____　____　____　　B. At some point during the course of the disorder, the person has recognized that the obsessions or compulsions are excessive or unreasonable. NOTE: This does not apply to children.

____   ____   ____   C. The obsessions or compulsions cause marked distress, are time-consuming (take more than one hour a day), or significantly interfere with the person's normal routine, occupational (or academic) functioning, or usual social activities or relationships.

Name _____ Date _____

Self-Rating Report of Panic Symptoms

0————————————1—————————————————————————10

Not significant   Present a small amount   As severe as
most of the time.   most of the time to a   possible.
                         significant degree.

Panic Attack: A discrete period of intense fear or discomfort, in which four (or more) of the following symptoms developed abruptly and reached peak within ten minutes:

Past   Present Severity 0–10

Past	Present	Severity	
____	____	____	1. Palpitations, pounding heart, or accelerated heart rate
____	____	____	2. Sweating
____	____	____	3. Trembling or shaking
____	____	____	4. Sensations of shortness of breath or smothering
____	____	____	5. Feeling of choking
____	____	____	6. Chest pain or discomfort
____	____	____	7. Nausea or abdominal distress
____	____	____	8. Feeling dizzy, unsteady, lightheaded, or faint
____	____	____	9. Derealization (feeling of unreality) or depersonalization (being detached from oneself)
____	____	____	10. Fear of losing control or going crazy
____	____	____	11. Fear of dying
____	____	____	12. Chills or hot flashes

Name _____ Date _____

Self-Rating Report of Post-traumatic Stress Disorder (PTSD) Symptoms

0————————1——————————————————10

| Not significant most of the time. | Present a small amount most of the time to a significant degree. | As severe as possible. |

Past   Present Severity 0–10

____ ____ ____   A. The person has been exposed to a traumatic event in which both of the following were present:
1. The person experienced, witnessed, or was confronted with an event or events that involved actual or threatened death or serious injury, or a threat to the physical integrity of self or others.

____ ____ ____   2. The person's response involved intense fear, helplessness, or horror. NOTE: In children, this may be expressed instead by disorganized or agitated behavior.

B. The traumatic event is persistently reexperienced in one (or more) of the following ways:

____ ____ ____   1. Recurrent and intrusive distressing recollections of the event, including images, thoughts, or perceptions. NOTE: In young children, repetitive play may occur in which themes or aspects of the trauma are expressed.

____ ____ ____   2. Recurrent distressing dreams of the event. NOTE: In children, there may be frightening dreams without recognizable content.

____ ____ ____   3. Acting or feeling as if the traumatic event were recurring (includes a sense of reliving the experience, illusions, hallucinations, and dissociative flashback episodes, including those that occur on awakening or when intoxicated). NOTE: In young children, trauma-specific reenactment may occur.

____ ____ ____   4. Intense psychological distress at exposure to internal or external cues that symbolize or resemble an aspect of the traumatic event.

____ ____ ____   5. Physiological reactivity on exposure to internal or external cues that symbolize or resemble an aspect of the traumatic event.

C. Persistent avoidance of stimuli associated with the trauma and numbing of general responsiveness (not present before the trauma), as indicated by three (or more) of the following:

____ ____ ____   1. Efforts to avoid thoughts, feelings, or conversations associated with the trauma.

____ ____ ____   2. Efforts to avoid activities, places, or people that arouse recollections of the trauma.

____ ____ ____   3. Inability to recall an important aspect of the trauma.

____ ____ ____   4. Markedly diminished interest or participation in significant activities.

____ ____ ____   5. Feeling of detachment or estrangement from others.

____ ____ ____   6. Restricted range of affect (e.g., unable to have loving feelings).

____ ____ ____   7. Sense of a foreshortened future (e.g., does not expect to have a career, marriage, children, or a normal life span).

D. Persistent symptoms of increased arousal (not present before the trauma), as indicated by two (or more) of the following:

____ ____ ____   1. Difficulty falling or staying asleep.

____ ____ ____   2. Irritability or outbursts of anger.

____ ____ ____   3. Difficulty concentrating.

____ ____ ____   4. Hypervigilance.

____ ____ ____   5. Exaggerated startle response.

____ ____ ____   E. Duration of the disturbance (symptoms in Criteria B, C, and D) is more than one month.

____ ____ ____   F. The disturbance causes clinically significant distress or impairment in social, occupational, or other important areas of functioning.

Name _____ Date _____

Self-Rating Report of Social Phobia (Social Anxiety Disorder) Symptoms

0————————————1——————————————————————10

Not significant   Present a small amount   As severe as
most of the time.   most of the time to a   possible.
                         significant degree.

Past Present Severity 0–10

____   ____   ____   A. A marked and persistent fear of one or more social or per-
formance situations in which the person is exposed to unfa-
miliar people or to possible scrutiny by others. The individual
fears that he or she will act in a way (or show anxiety symptoms) that will be humiliating or embarrassing. NOTE: In children, there must be evidence of the capacity for age-appropri-
ate social relationships with familiar people, and the anxiety
must occur in peer settings, not just in interactions with adults.

____   ____   ____   B. Exposure to the feared social situation almost invariably pro-
vokes anxiety, which may take the form of a situationally bound
or situationally predisposed panic attack. NOTE: In children,
the anxiety may be expressed by crying, tantrums, freezing, or
shrinking from social situations with unfamiliar people.

____   ____   ____   C. The person recognized that the fear is excessive or unreason-
able. NOTE: In children, this feature may be absent.

____   ____   ____   D. The feared social or performance situations are avoided or else
are endured with intense anxiety or distress.

____   ____   ____   E. The avoidance, anxious anticipation, or distress in the feared
social or performance situation(s) interferes significantly with
the person's normal routine, occupational (academic) functioning, or social activities or relationships, or there is marked
distress about having the phobia.

Name _____ Date _____

Self-Rating Report of Specific Phobia Symptoms

0————————1————————————————10

Not significant   Present a small amount   As severe as
most of the time.   most of the time to a   possible.
      significant degree.

Past   Present Severity 0–10

____ ____ ____   A. Marked and persistent fear that is excessive or unreasonable, cued by the presence or anticipation of a specific object or situation (e.g., flying, heights, animals, receiving an injection, seeing blood).

____ ____ ____   B. Exposure to the phobic stimulus almost invariably provokes an immediate anxiety response, which may take the form of a situationally bound or situationally predisposed panic attack. NOTE: In children, the anxiety may be expressed by crying, tantrums, freezing, or clinging.

____ ____ ____   C. The person recognizes that the fear is excessive or unreasonable. NOTE: In children this feature may be absent.

____ ____ ____   D. The phobic situation(s) is avoided or else is endured with intense anxiety or distress.

____ ____ ____   E. The avoidance, anxious anticipation, or distress in the feared situation(s) interferes significantly with the person's normal routine, occupational (or academic) functioning, or social activities or relationships, or there is marked distress about having the phobia.

Skills of the Christian Counselor

The Christian counselor must develop a variety of skills if he is to be of service to his counselees. These abilities are essential throughout the counseling process—from the initial interview through final resolution of the problem. In this section we will touch on a number of these skills. The counselor should periodically evaluate how he measures up in each of these areas. It is often beneficial to have a colleague join in this evaluation.

The Ability to Obtain Data

If the counselor is to be successful, he must be able to obtain enough data to make judgments concerning both the nature of the problem and suitable treatment. Central to this is keen observation of any symptoms the counselee may manifest. In addition to general appearance, any abnormalities such as disorientation, delusions, hallucinations, obsessions, phobias, or thought disturbances are to be noted. The counselor will try to get a sense of the counselee's moods and interpersonal relationships.

To get a correct perspective of the counselee, it is essential to develop the art of asking the right question. This includes knowing how to raise and deal with the results of provocative, anxiety-arousing questions, as well as how to move from general to specific questions. The counselor must also develop the art of logically and discreetly steering the interview into difficult and painful areas (previous psychiatric problems, drug or alcohol abuse, suicide attempts). In addition, it is important to be able to explain terms clearly (e.g., "depression"), to follow up leads, and to end the interview tactfully.

The Ability to Formulate an Approach

Choosing from among the great variety of approaches and plans of action that can be adopted with respect to any individual counselee is one of the most difficult tasks confronted by the counselor. How is the novice counselor to know how to proceed? Our advice is for him to utilize a few basic techniques as he gets started. He will learn to vary his approach to meet the particular needs of his counselees as his experience, knowledge, and sensitivity increase. He must be patient with himself as he tries to master the complex world of counseling with its many dimensions. He will with time learn when to provide insight and when to offer support, when to emphasize behavior and when to focus on feelings, when to be direct and when to be indirect, when to delve into the past and when to concentrate on the present. He will also learn the importance of being himself. The counselee will have confidence in him only if he is spontaneous and nondefensive.

The difficulty of knowing how to select the right approach is underscored by the great number of options available. We can present here only a very brief general list of what the counselor can do:

1. *Offer support.* Supportive counseling is emotional and spiritual backing. Among the techniques falling under this general heading are advice (Prov. 19:20), comfort (2 Cor. 1:3–4), encouragement (Rom. 1:11–12), listening (Elihu in Job 32), and education (the letters of Paul). Supportive counseling is, of course, not limited to private sessions. The whole body of Christ has great potential as a source of support for people in need of help.

2. *Provide insight.* The parables of Christ enlightened his audiences to truths about themselves that they would not otherwise have perceived. Nathan the prophet used a similar approach to make David aware of his sin.

3. *Urge confession* (James 5:16).

4. *Give positive verbal reinforcement* (Rom. 1:8).

5. *Present a Christian example.* Many biblical personalities modeled godly conduct to others. Recall Moses' example to Joshua, Naomi's example to Ruth, Christ's example to his disciples.

6. *Educate the counselee;* that is, challenge his false beliefs (Gal. 4:9). The Christian counselor can offer God's truths in their stead. A most useful procedure in this case is to give the counselee homework assignments.

7. *Work with the client in a group setting.* Scripture frequently emphasizes the importance and personal benefits of interaction with others—love one another, bear one another's burdens, be ye kind to one another (1 Cor.; Eph. 4:14–16).

8. *Begin a counseling program with the client's family.* There is a strong emphasis on the family in both the Old and New Testaments. The apostle Paul gave much advice on family life (Eph. 5:22–33; 6:1–4).

9. *Utilize modern techniques for improving behavior.* Among the techniques available are assertiveness training, behavior rehearsal, and positive and negative reinforcement.

We have up to this point touched only the surface. Among other plans of action which the counselor can adopt are mediated catharsis, admonishment (1 Thess. 5:14), confrontation, and urging the counselee to reflection or self-disclosure.

In many instances the counselor will find that one method or approach is insufficient. Support alone may not be enough. Insight alone may not be enough (Solomon had much insight but still fell into sin). Likewise, listening or catharsis alone may have little impact on the counselee's life. There need to be specific behavioral changes. Scripture repeatedly emphasizes the importance of proper Christian activity (Matt. 7:24; Phil. 2:13; 4:13). If there is little or no change for the better in the counselee's behavior within a reasonable time, some additional approach(es) should be adopted. In such cases we have often found it helpful for the counselee to examine his own plan for life (i.e., to take a close look at the way he is actually living). Then we assist him to make appropriate changes. We call this going from plan A to plan B. Plan B recommends specific daily activities that will produce health. Among the recommendations are social interactions, exercise, recreation, and a quiet time. This plan needs to be explicit and should be reevaluated periodically.

If all of this should prove inadequate, the counselor will recognize that additional factors may be involved and that further evaluation is necessary. There may be a need for specialized psychological tests. Or referral of the counselee for an extensive physical exam, psychiatric medication, or hospitalization may be called for.

Modeling Christlike Attitudes

It is essential that the Christian counselor make a conscious effort to be like Christ. The more closely the counselor patterns his manner of dealing with clients after the manner in which Jesus dealt with the people of his time, the more successful he will be. One of the most striking features of Jesus' ministry is the variety of attitudes he displayed. At times he was gentle and passive. On other occasions he was active and friendly or kind but firm. If the circumstances warranted, he could be downright stern. In other words, Jesus adapted himself to the specific situation. So should the Christian counselor (see 1 Thess. 5:14).

Reflecting Christ's ministry, the hallmarks of Christian counseling are kindness and gentleness (2 Cor. 1:3–4; 10:1; Gal. 6:1; 1 Thess. 2:7, 11; 2 Tim. 2:24; Titus 3:2). The most obvious sign of Christ's ministering to and through the Christian counselor will be the love he shows to his clients. Remember that love is a major emphasis of Scripture: "Though I speak with the tongues of men and of angels, and have not charity, I am become as sounding brass, or a tinkling cymbal" (1 Cor. 13:1 KJV); "But the fruit of the Spirit is love, joy, peace, longsuffering, gentleness, goodness, faith, meekness, temperance: against such there is no law" (Gal. 5:22–23 KJV).

The counselor's efforts to model a Christlike attitude will be evident from the initial contact through every aspect of the counseling process. By adopting a Christlike approach, the counselor will be able to put the counselee at ease, establish rapport, set a tone of honesty for the interview, and show compassion, concern, and empathy. Such a counselor will be responsive to variations in the counselee's mood. He will be flexible in dealing with difficult situations (e.g., if the counselee refuses to talk or is obviously paranoid), avoid any show of great surprise, and maintain an appropriate level of eye contact. He will be sensitive to such seemingly small matters as the physical setting (e.g., the placement of the chairs) and his body position (he will lean slightly forward to demonstrate interest). The communication will be on a level the counselee can understand. The counselor who patterns his approach after Christ's will develop acute listening skills (James 1:19) and will be able to elicit pertinent information tactfully.

The Ability to Use Scripture

Scripture plays a crucial role in Christian counseling. By providing spiritual nourishment, God's Word produces growth and healing in the counselee. The Christian counselor will use the Bible with discernment, tact, and sensitivity. There are many ways in which the counselor can use God's Word, for example, as a means of direct challenge and confrontation, or as a source of encouragement and positive reinforcement. The Bible also offers practical advice and numerous models of godly lives. Under appropriate circumstances the counselor might consider giving homework assignments (Bible study and/or memorization). Or he might help the counselee by pointing out passages which have been of special benefit in his own personal life. With experience the counselor will discover more and more ways to use the Bible.

We have seen that there are a number of requisites for successful Christian counseling. They include skill in obtaining data, the ability to formulate an approach suitable for the individual counselee, a Christlike attitude, and knowledge of how to use Scripture. The wise counselor will evaluate himself periodically and strive earnestly for improvement in those areas where he falls short.

Spiritual Consequences of Physical and Emotional Problems

Physical and Emotional Problems Can Affect Spiritual Life

Another indication that the various dimensions of man's nature are inextricably interrelated is the fact that certain physical and emotional problems have real or apparent effects on one's spiritual life. Individuals with temporal-lobe epilepsy may experience a renewed interest in religion and display a moral piety. Someone on the brink of a psychotic breakdown may be preoccupied by religious matters. A person with an obsessive-compulsive neurosis may fear that he has committed the unpardonable sin or that he does not have a sufficient trust in Christ. Manic-depressives may talk in a religious jargon. While schizophrenics and multiple personalities may be thought to be demon possessed, they are not. Proof of this is their response to antipsychotic medication. (See the chart below for a list of physical and emotional factors which affect spiritual life.)

Physical and Emotional Factors with Spiritual Consequences

There are a number of physical and emotional factors that have real or apparent effects on spiritual life:

1. *Temporal-lobe epilepsy* may result in heightened religious interest and perfectionistic tendencies. Individuals with temporal-lobe epilepsy may go from church to church, considering none of them good enough. In this case the problem is physical rather than spiritual.

---

2. *Drugs* have long been associated with "religious" experience.

3. *Defense mechanisms* such as denial, introjection, and projection may cause a person to appear superreligious when in fact he is not.

4. *Psychosis* may involve a religious preoccupation. This is a result of an increase in abstract thinking rather than true spirituality.

5. *Manic-depressive disorder* causes some of its victims to talk in a religious jargon.

6. *Obsessive-compulsive neurosis* may involve constant worries that one is not saved or has committed the unpardonable sin. These worries mask the underlying conflicts (with one's parents or mate). There may also be a defect in the circuits of the central nervous system. The result is a religious obsession, an oppressive thought that cannot be dislodged. An apt comparison is a record player stuck in one groove.

RESOURCE W

Staff and Systems

Staff and systems vary widely. Many systems today consist of no extra staff. The therapist makes appointments, does therapy, collects fees, answers the phone, and does his or her own public relations. Other systems are extensive with medical doctors, nurses, counselors, a receptionist to greet clients, a receptionist to answer the phone, billing department, insurance department, director of public relations, intake department, typist, administrator, and executive director. Other systems consist of an approach between these two.

Bibliography

Adams, Jay E. *The Use of Scriptures in Counseling*. Grand Rapids: Baker, 1975.

Adams, Jay. *Competent to Counsel*. Grand Rapids: Baker, 1970.

Adler, Charles S., Sheila Morrissey Adler, and Russell C. Packard. *Psychiatric Aspects of Headache*. Baltimore: Williams & Wilkins, 1987.

Albers, Lawrence J., Rhoda K. Hahn, Christopher Reist. *Current Clinical Strategies: Handbook of Psychiatric Drugs*. Laguna Hills, Calif.: Current Clinical Strategies Publishing, 2001.

Allen, Charles L. *God's Psychiatry*. Old Tappan; N.J.: Fleming H. Revell, 1953.

Allen, James R. and Barbara Ann Allen. *Guide to Psychiatry*. New York: Medical Examination Publishing Co., 1978.

American Psychiatric Association. *Quick Reference to the Diagnostic Criteria from DSM-IV*. Washington, D.C.: American Psychiatric Association, 1994.

American Psychiatric Association 2001 Annual Meeting New Research Abstracts. Washington, D.C.: American Psychiatric Association, 2001.

Andreasen, Nancy D. and Donald W. Black. *Introductory Textbook of Psychiatry*, 2nd ed. Washington, D.C.: American Psychiatric Press, 1995.

Arky, Ronald. *2001 Physician's Desk Reference*. Montvale: Medical Economics Company, 1997.

Bainton, Roland H. *Here I Stand, a Life of Martin Luther*. New York: Mentor Books, 1950.

Bannister, Roger. *Brain's Clinical Neurology*, 5th ed. Oxford: Oxford University Press, 1978.

Barker, Kenneth, ed. *The NIV Study Bible*. Grand Rapids: Zondervan, 1985.

Beers, Mark H., and Robert Berkow, eds. *The Merck Manual of Diagnosis and Therapy*, 17th ed. Whitehouse Station: Merck Research Laboratories, 1999.

Beeson, Paul B. and Walsh McDermott, eds. *Textbook of Medicine*, 13th ed. Philadelphia: W. B. Saunders Company, 1971.

Benjamin, Ludy T., Jr., J. Roy Hopkins, and Jack R. Nation. *Psychology*, 3rd ed. New York: McMillan Publishing Company, 1994.

Benson, Bob, Sr., and Michael W. Benson. *Disciplines for the Inner Life*. Nashville: Generoux/Nelson, 1989.

Bergin, James D. *Medicine Recall*. Baltimore: Lippincott Wiliams & Wilkins, 1997.

Berkhof, Louis. *Systematic Theology.* Carlisle: Banner of Truth Trust, 1958.

Bernstein, Carol A., Brian J. Ladds, Ann S. Maloney, and Elyse D. Weiner. *On Call Psychiatry.* Philadelphia: W. B. Saunders Company, 2001, 1997.

Berry, George R. *The Interlinear Greek-English New Testament with Lexicon and Synonyms.* Grand Rapids: Zondervan, 1976.

Bounds, E. M. *Power Through Prayer.* Grand Rapids: Baker Book House, 1991.

Bounds, E. M. *The Weapon of Prayer.* New Kensington: Whitaker House, 1996.

Brandt, Henry R. and Homer E. Dowdy. *Christians Have Troubles Too.* Old Tappan; N.J.: Fleming H. Revell, 1968.

Braunwald, Eugene, Kurt J. Isselbacher, Jean D. Wilson, Joseph B. Martin, Anthony S. Fauci, and Dennis Kasper, eds. *Harrison's Principles of Internal Medicine,* 13th ed. New York: McGraw-Hill Book Company, 1994.

Braunwald, Eugene, Kurt J. Isselbacher, Jean D. Wilson, Joseph B. Martin, Anthony S. Fauci, Dennis Kasper, Stephen Hauser, and Dan Longo, eds. *Harrison's Principles of Internal Medicine—Companion Handbook,* 14th ed. New York: McGraw-Hill Book Company, 1998.

Brown, Colin, ed. *The New International Dictionary of New Testament Theology,* Vol. 1–3. Grand Rapids: Zondervan, 1979.

Brown, Thomas E., ed. *Attention-Deficit Disorders and Comorbidities in Children, Adolescents, and Adults.* Washington, D.C.: American Psychiatric Press, 2000.

Bullock, C. Hassell. *An Introduction to the Old Testament Poetic Books.* Chicago: Moody Press, 1979.

Burnside, John W. *Adam's Physical Diagnosis—an Introduction to Clinical Medicine,* 15th ed. Baltimore: Williams & Wilkins, 1974.

Campbell, Donald K. *Nehemiah: Man in Charge.* Wheaton: Victor Books, 1979.

Carey, Charles F., Hans H. Lee, and Keith F. Woeltje, eds. *The Washington Manual of Medical Therapeutics,* 29th ed. Philadelphia: Lippincott-Raven Publishers, 1998.

Carlson, Neil R. *Psychology—The Science of Behavior.* Boston: Allyn and Bacon, 1990.

Carter, John D. "Secular and Sacred Models of Psychology and Religion." *Journal of Psychology and Theology* (1977): 197–208.

Carter, Les. *People Pleasers.* Nashville: Broadman & Holman Publishers, 2000.

Chafer, Lewis Sperry. *God's Marvelous Work of Grace—Salvation.* Grand Rapids: Kregel Publications, 1991.

Chafer, Lewis Sperry. *Grace, the Glorious Theme.* Grand Rapids: Academie Books/Zondervan, 1950.

Chafer, Lewis Sperry. *Major Bible Themes.* Grand Rapids: Zondervan, 1974.

Chafer, Lewis Sperry. *Systematic Theology,* Vol. 1–8. Dallas: Dallas Seminary Press, 1948.

Chapin, Alice. *365 Bible Promises for People Who Worry.* Wheaton: Tyndale House Publishers, 1998.

Charney, Dennis S., Eric J. Nestler, and Benjamin S. Bunny, eds. *Neurobiology of Mental Illness.* Oxford: Oxford University Press, 1999.

Chatton, Milton J. *Handbook of Medical Treatment,* 16th ed. Greenbrae: Jones Medical Publications, 1979.

Chessell, G. S. J., M. J. Jamieson, R. A. Morton, J. C. Petrie, and H. M. A. Towler. *Photo Dx: An Aid for the Study of Clinical Diagnosis,* Vol. 1–4. Chicago: Year Book Medical Publishers, 1984.

Cheydleur, John R. *Called to Counsel.* Wheaton: Tyndale House Publishers, 1999.

Clark, Ronald G. *Manter and Gatz's Essentials of Clinical Neuroanatomy and Neurophysiology,* 5th ed. Philadelphia: F. A. Davis, 1975.

Clayman, Charles B., ed. *The American Medical Association Encyclopedia of Medicine.* New York: Random House, 1989.

Coleman, Robert E. *The Master Plan of Evangelism.* Old Tappan; N.J.: Fleming H. Revell Company, 1964.

Collins, Gary R. *Christian Counseling, a Comprehensive Guide.* Dallas: Word Publishing, 1988.

Collins, Gary R. *The Christian Psychology of Paul Tournier.* Grand Rapids: Baker, 1973.

Collins, Gary R. *Innovative Approaches to Counseling.* Dallas: Word Publishing, 1986.

Collins, Gary. *Man in Motion.* Carol Stream: Creation House, 1973.

Collins, Gary. *Man in Transition.* Carol Stream: Creation House, 1971.

Collins, Gary. *Overcoming Anxiety.* Santa Ana, Calif.: Vision House Publishers, 1973.

Collins, Gary. *Search for Reality—Psychology and the Christian.* Wheaton: Key Publishers, 1969.

Conners, C. Keith and Juliet L. Jett. *Attention Deficit Hyperactivity Disorder (In Adults and Children)— the Latest Assessment and Treatment Strategies.* Kansas City: Compact Clinicals, 1999.

Corsini, Raymond J. *Handbook of Innovative Psychotherapies.* New York: John Wiley & Sons, 1981.

Cosgrove, Mark P. and James D. Mallory Jr. *Mental Health: A Christian Approach.* Grand Rapids: Zondervan, 1977.

Covert, Cathy, ed. *Mental Retardation, a Handbook for the Primary Physician.* Chicago: American Medical Association, 1965.

Crabb, Larry. *Effective Biblical Counseling.* Grand Rapids: Zondervan Publishing House, 1977.

Criders, Andrew B., George R. Goethals, Robert D. Kavanaugh, and Paul R. Solomon. *Psychology,* 3rd ed. Glenview: Scott, Foresman and Company, 1989.

Csillag, Andras. *Anatomy of the Living Human.* Koln: Konemann, 1999.

Dake, Finis Jennings. *Dake's Annotated Reference Bible.* Lawrenceville: Dake Bible Sales, Inc., 1963.

Davis, John J. *Conquest and Crisis, Studies in Joshua, Judges, and Ruth.* Grand Rapids: Baker Book House, 1969.

Design for Discipleship—a Bible Study Series. Colorado Springs: The Navigators, 1973.

DiCaprio, Nicholas S. *Personality Theories: Guides to Living.* Philadelphia: W. B. Saunders Company, 1974.

Dillow, Linda. *Creative Counterpart.* Nashville: Thomas Nelson, 1977.

Dobson, James. *Hide or Seek—How to Build Self Esteem in Your Child.* Old Tappan, N.J.: Fleming H. Revell, 1979.

Dobson, James C. *Straight Talk to Men and Their Wives.* Waco: Tyndale House Publishers, 1998.

Douglas, J. D., ed. *The New Bible Dictionary.* Grand Rapids: Eerdmans, 1962.

Dubovsky, Steven L. *Clinical Psychiatry.* Washington, D.C.: American Psychiatric Press, 1988.

Dunnett, Walter. *An Outline of New Testament Survey.* Chicago: Moody Press, 1960.

Edman, V. Raymond. *The Disciplines of Life.* Minneapolis: World Wide Publications, 1948.

Ellicott, Charles John. *Ellicott's Bible Commentary in One Volume.* Grand Rapids: Zondervan, 1971.

Ellicott, Charles John, ed. *Ellicott's Commentary on the Whole Bible.* Grand Rapids: Zondervan, 1981.

Erickson, Millard J. *Christian Theology,* 2nd ed. Grand Rapids: Baker Books, 1998.

Ewald, Gregory A. and Clark R. McKenzie, eds. *The Washington Manual—Manual of Medical Therapeutics,* 29th ed. Boston: Little, Brown and Company, 1995.

Fadem, Barbara and Steven Simring. *Psychiatry Recall.* Baltimore: Williams & Wilkins, 1997.

Feldman, Robert S. *Essentials of Understanding Psychology.* New York: McGraw-Hill, 1989.

Feltman, John, ed. *Prevention's Giant Book of Health Facts.* Emmaus: Rodale Press, 1991.

First, Michael B., ed. *Diagnostic and Statistical Manual of Mental Disorders,* 4th ed. Washington, D.C.: American Psychiatric Association, 1994.

Flaherty, Joseph A., John M. Davis, and Philip G. Janicak, eds. *Psychiatry—Diagnosis and Treatment,* 2nd ed. Norwalk: Appleton & Lange, 1993.

Forster, Francis M. *Clinical Neurology,* 3rd ed. St. Louis: The C. V. Mosby Company, 1973.

Fowler, Richard A. *Winning by Losing.* Chicago: Moody Press, 1986.

Freedman, Alfred M. and Harold I. Kaplan. *The Child—His Psychological and Cultural Development.* New York: Atheneum, 1972.

Gaebelein, Frank E., ed. *The Expositor's Bible Commentary.* Grand Rapids: Zondervan, 1981.

Gitlin, Michael J. *The Psychotherapist's Guide to Psychopharmacology,* 2nd ed. New York: The Free Press, 1996.

Goldberger, Leo and Shlomo Breznitz, eds. *Handbook of Stress—Theoretical and Clinical Aspects.* New York: The Free Press, 1982.

Goldman, H. H., ed. *Review of General Psychiatry,* 2nd ed. Los Altos: Lange Medical Publications, 1988.

Good, William V. and Jefferson E. Nelson. *Psychiatry Made Ridiculously Simple,* 2nd ed. Miami: MedMaster Inc., 1991.

Goodrick, Edward W., John R. Kohlenberger III. *Zondervan NIV Exhaustive Concordance,* 2nd ed. Grand Rapids: Zondervan, 1999.

Grudem, Wayne. *Systematic Theology.* Grand Rapids: Zondervan, 1994.

Guyton, Arthur C. *Textbook of Medical Physiology.* Philadelphia: W. B. Saunders Company, 1991.

Hahn, Rhonda K., Christopher Reist, and Lawrence J. Albers. *Psychiatry 1999–2000 Edition.* Laguna Hills: Current Clinical Strategies, 2000.

Haist, Steve A., John B. Robbins, and Leonard G. Gomella. *Internal Medicine on Call.* Norwalk: Appleton & Lange, 1991.

Harrison, R. K. *Leviticus, An Introduction and Commentary.* Downers Grove: InterVarsity Press, 1980.

Hendricks, Howard G. *Heaven Help the Home!* Wheaton: Victor Books, 1975.

Henry, Matthew and Thomas Scott. *Commentary on the Holy Bible.* Nashville: Thomas Nelson, 1979.

Herink, Richie, ed. *The Psychotherapy Handbook.* New York: A Meridian Book/New American Library, 1980.

Hindson, Ed and Walter Byrd. *When the Road Gets Rough.* Tarrytown: Fleming H. Revell, 1986.

Hollander, Eric and Cheryl M. Wong. *Contemporary Diagnosis and Management of Common Psychiatric Disorders.* Newton: Handbooks in Health Care Co., 2000.

Hyman, Steven E., George W. Arana, and Jerrold F. Rosenbaum. *Handbook of Psychiatric Drug Therapy,* 3rd ed. Boston: Little, Brown and Company, 1995.

Ironside, H. A. *Full Assurance.* Chicago: Moody Press, 1937.

Jacob, Leonard S. *Pharmacology,* 4th ed. Baltimore: Williams & Wilkins, 1996.

Janicak, Philip G. *Handbook of Psychopharmacotherapy.* Baltimore: Lippincott Williams & Wilkins, 1999.

Jersild, Arthur T., Judith S. Brook, and David W. Brook. *The Psychology of Adolescence,* 3rd ed. New York: McMillan, 1979.

Johnson, Cecil. *Ruth (An Exposition).* Rocky Mount: Christian Bible College, 1982.

Johnson, L. D. *An Introduction to the Bible.* Nashville: Convention Press, 1969.

Kaplan, Harold I. and Benjamin J. Sadock. *Comprehensive Textbook of Psychiatry,* 7th ed., Vol. 1 and 2. Baltimore: Lippincott, Williams & Wilkins, 2000.

Kaplan, Harold I. and Benjamin J. Sadock. *Pocket Handbook of Primary Care Psychiatry.* Baltimore: Williams & Wilkins, 1996.

Kaplan, Harold I., and Benjamin J. Sadock. *Pocket Handbook of Psychiatric Treatment,* 2nd ed. Baltimore: Williams and Wilkins, 1996.

Karaus, Toksoz B. "Psychotherapies: An Overview." *American Journal of Psychiatry* 134.8 (1977): 851–63.

Kaufman, David Myland. *Clinical Neurology for Psychiatrists,* 3rd ed. Philadelphia: W. B. Saunders Company, 1990.

Keck, Paul and Susan McElroy. *Overview of CNS Disorders 2001.* New York: McMahon Publishing Group, 2000.

Kirchheimer, Sid. *The Doctors Book of Home Remedies II.* New York: Bantam Books, 1995.

Kleinmuntz, Benjamin. *Essentials of Abnormal Psychology.* New York: Harper & Row, 1974.

Knight, Walter B. *Knight's Master Book of New Illustrations.* Grand Rapids: Eerdmans, 1956.

Knight, Walter B. *Knight's Timely Illustrations.* Murfreesboro: Sword of the Lord Publishers, 1984.

Krupp, Marcus A., Lawrence M. Tierney Jr., Ernest Jawetz, Robert L. Roe, and Carlos A. Camargo. *Physician's Handbook,* 21st ed. Los Altos: Lange Medical Publications, 1982.

LaHaye, Tim. *The Battle for the Family.* Old Tappan, N.J.: Fleming H. Revell, 1982.

LaHaye, Tim. *How to Win over Depression.* Grand Rapids: Zondervan, 1974.

Lee, Witness. *The Economy of God.* Los Angeles: The Stream Publishers, 1968.

Leonard, Brian E. *Fundamentals of Psychopharmacology,* 2nd ed. Chichester: Wiley, 1997.

Lewis, Melvin, ed. *Child and Adolescent Psychiatry, A Comprehensive Textbook.* Baltimore: Williams & Wilkins, 1991.

Lezak, Muriel Deutsch. *Neuropsychological Assessment,* 3rd ed. Oxford: Oxford University Press, 1995.

Little, Paul E. *Know What You Believe.* Wheaton: Scripture Press Publications, 1970.

Long, Donlin M. *Contemporary Diagnosis and Management of Pain,* 2nd ed. Newtown: Handbooks in Health Care Co., 2000.

Lullmann, Heinz, Klaus Mohr, Albrecht Ziegler, and Detlef Bieger. *Color Atlas of Pharmacology.* New York: Thieme Medical Publishers Inc., 1993.

Mabbett, Phyllis D. *Instant Nursing Assessment: Mental Health.* Albany: Delmar Publishers, 1996.

MacDonald, William. *Believer's Bible Commentary.* Nashville: Thomas Nelson, 1990.

Margulies, David M. and Malcolm S. Thaler. *The Physician's Book of Lists.* New York: Churchill Livingstone, 1983.

Marieb, Elaine N. *Human Anatomy and Physiology.* Redwood City: The Benjamin Cummings Publishing Company, 1992.

McCarthy, Malia, Mary B. O'Malley, and Sanjay Saint. *Saint-Frances Guide to Psychiatry.* Baltimore: Lippincott Williams & Wilkins, 2001.

McDowell, Josh. *Evidence That Demands a Verdict,* Vol. 1 and 2. Nashville: Thomas Nelson, 1993.

McGee, Robert S. *The Search for Significance.* Nashville: Word Publishing, 1998.

McKinney, B. B. *The Broadman Hymnal.* Nashville: The Broadman Press, 1940.

McMinn, Mark R. *Psychology, Theology, and Spirituality in Christian Counseling.* Wheaton: Tyndale Publishing House, 1996.

McNeil, Elton B. and Zick Rubin. *The Psychology of Being Human.* San Francisco: Canfield Press, 1977.

Mead, Frank S., ed. *12,000 Religious Quotations.* Grand Rapids: Baker, 1989.

Miller, Basil W. *The Gold Under the Grass.* Nashville: Cokesbury Press, 1930.

Miller, James and Nathan Fountain. *Neurology Recall.* Baltimore: Williams & Wilkins, 1997.

Morgan, Clifford T., Richard A. King, John R. Weisz, and John Schopler. *Introduction to Psychology,* 7th ed. New York: McGraw-Hill, 1986.

Morris, Paul D. *Love Therapy.* Wheaton: Tyndale House Publishers, 1974.

Murray, Andrew. *The New Life.* Minneapolis: Bethany Fellowship, Inc., 1965.

Narramore, Bruce and Bill Counts. *Freedom from Guilt.* Santa Ana: Vision House Publishers, 1974.

Nave, Orville J. *The New Nave's Topical Bible.* Grand Rapids: Regency Reference Library at Zondervan House, 1969.

Nee, Watchman. *Christ, the Sum of All Spiritual Things.* New York: Christian Fellowship Publishers, Inc., 1973.

Nee, Watchman. *The Normal Christian Worker.* Hong Kong: Church Book Room,1965.

Nee, Watchman. *Sit, Walk, Stand.* Wheaton: Tyndale House Publishers, 1977.

Nee, Watchman. *The Spiritual Man,* Vol. 1–3. New York: Christian Fellowship Publishers, Inc. 1968.

Nemeroff, Charles B. and Thomas W. Uhde, ed. *Depression and Anxiety,* Vol. 12. New York: Wiley-Liss, 2000.

Nicholl, W. Robertson, ed. *The Expositor's Greek Testament,* Vols. I through V. Grand Rapids: Eerdmans, 1980.

Nicoli, Armand M., Jr., ed. *The New Harvard Guide to Psychiatry.* Cambridge: The Belknap Press of Harvard University Press, 1988.

Olson, William H., Roger A. Brumback, Iyer Vasudeva, and Generso Gascon. *Handbook of Symptom-Oriented Neurology.* St. Louis: Mosby, 1994.

Osbeck, Kenneth W. *101 Hymn Stories.* Grand Rapids: Kregel Publications, 1982.

Osbeck, Kenneth W. *101 More Hymn Stories.* Grand Rapids: Kregel Publications, 1985.

Peale, Norman Vincent. *The Power of Positive Thinking.* New York: Fawcett Crest, 1956.

Pentecost, Dwight J. *Design for Discipleship.* Grand Rapids: Kregel Publications, 1996.

Peterson, Jim. *Lifestyle Discipleship.* Colorado Springs: NavPress, 1993.

Preston, John, and James Johnson. *Clinical Psychopharmacology Made Ridiculously Simple.* Miami: MedMaster, Inc., 1993.

Ramachandran, Anand. *Pharmacology Recall.* Baltimore: Lippincott Williams & Wilkins, 2000.

Rassmussen, S. A., J. L. Eisen, and M. T. Pato. "Current Issues in the Pharmacological Management of Obsessive Compulsive Disorder." *Journal of Clinical Psychiatry* (1993): 4–9.

Restak, Richard M. *The Brain.* Toronto: Bantam Books, 1984.

Restak, Richard M. *The Modular Brain.* New York: Charles Scribner's Sons, 1994.

Ruedy, Giles Marshall. *On Call—Principles and Protocols.* Philadelphia: W. B. Saunders Co., 1989.

Rutter, Michael, Eric Taylor, and Lionel Hersov, eds. *Child and Adolescent Psychiatry, Modern Approaches.* Oxford: Blackwell Scientific Publications, 1994.

Ryle, J. C. *Ryle's Expository Thoughts on the Gospels,* Vol. 1–4. Grand Rapids: Baker Book House, 1977.

Ryrie, Charles C. *Biblical Theology of the New Testament.* Chicago: Moody Press, 1959.

Ryrie, Charles C. *So Great Salvation.* Wheaton: Victor Books, 1989.

Ryrie, Charles Caldwell, ed. *The Ryrie Study Bible, KJV.* Chicago: Moody Press, 1978.

Ryrie, Charles Caldwell. *A Survey of Bible Doctrine.* Chicago: Moody Press, 1972.

Schaeffer, Francis A. *The God Who Is There.* Downers Grove: InterVarsity Press, 1968.

Schuller, Robert H. *Tough Times Never Last, but Tough People Do.* Nashville: Thomas Nelson, 1983.

Schultz, Samuel J. *The Old Testament Speaks,* 2nd ed. New York: Harper & Row, 1970.

Scofield, C. I., ed. *The New Scofield Study Bible.* Nashville: Thomas Nelson, 1982.

Scully, James H. *The National Medical Series for Independent Study: Psychiatry,* 3rd ed. Baltimore: Williams & Wilkins, 1996.

Shaner, Roderick. *Psychiatry—Board Review Series.* Baltimore: Williams & Wilkins, 1997.

Silver, Larry B. *Attention-Deficit Hyperactivity Disorder, a Clinical Guide to Diagnosis and Treatment.* Washington, D.C.: American Psychiatric Press, 1992.

Simpson, John F. and Kenneth R. Magee. *Clinical Evaluation of the Nervous System.* Boston: Little, Brown, and Company, 1973.

Smalley, Gary and John Trent. *The Blessing*. New York: Pocket Books, 1986.

Smith, Jerome H., ed. *The New Treasury of Scripture Knowledge*. Nashville: Thomas Nelson, 1992.

Sneed, Sharon M. and Joe S. McIlhaney. *PMS—What It Is and What You Can Do About It*. Grand Rapids: Baker Book House, 1988.

Solomon, Charles R. *Handbook of Happiness*. Denver: House of Solomon, 1971.

Stahl, Stephen M. *Essential Psychopharmacology, Neuroscientific Basis and Practical Applications*. Cambridge: Cambridge University Press, 1996.

Starlanyl, Devin and Mary Ellen Copeland. *Fibromyalgia & Chronic Myofascial Pain Syndrome, A Survival Manual*. Oakland: New Harbinger Publications, 1996.

Steegman, A. Theodore. *Examination of the Nervous System*. Chicago: Year Book Medical Publishers, 1970.

Stoop, David. *Self Talk: Key to Personal Growth*. Old Tappan; N.J.: Fleming H. Revell, 1982.

Stoop, Jan and David. *Saying Goodbye to Disappointments*. Nashville: Thomas Nelson, 1993.

Strong, James. *The New Strong's Exhaustive Concordance of the Bible*. Nashville: Thomas Nelson, 1984.

Tanner, Bradley T. and Janel Hanmer. *ADHD: A Guide for Families*. Pittsburgh, Penn.: Clinical Tools, Inc., 1998.

Taylor, Michael Alan. *The Neuropsychiatric Mental Status Examination*. New York: SP Medical and Scientific Books, 1981.

Tenney, Merrill C., ed. *The Zondervan Pictorial Encyclopedia of the Bible*. Grand Rapids: Zondervan, 1976.

Thieme, R. B. Jr., *The Biblical View of Sex, Love and Marriage*. Houston: Thieme, 1964.

Thies, Roger and Robert J. Person, eds. *Physiology*. New York: Springer-Verlag, 1987.

Thomas, Ian W. *The Saving Life of Christ*. Grand Rapids: Zondervan, 1961.

Tierney, Lawrence M., Jr, Stephen J. McPhee, and Maxine A. Papadakis. *2001 Current Medical Diagnosis & Treatment*. New York: Lange Medical Books/McGraw-Hill, 2001.

Tilkian, Sarko M., Mary Boudreau Conover, and Ara G. Tilkian. *Clinical Implications of Laboratory Tests*. St. Louis: The C. V. Mosby Company, 1996.

Timmons, Tim. *Maximum Marriage*. Old Tappan; N.J.: Fleming H. Revell, 1976.

Tomb, David A. *Psychiatry,* House Officer Series, 5th ed. Baltimore: Williams & Wilkins, 1995.

Tortora, Gerard J. and Sandra Reynolds Grabowski. *Principles of Anatomy and Physiology,* 8th ed. New York: Harper Collins, 1996.

Tozer, A. W. *The Knowledge of the Holy*. New York: Harper & Row, 1961.

Trobisch, Walter. *I Married You*. New York: Harper & Row, 1971.

Unger, Merril F. *Unger's Bible Handbook*. Chicago: Moody Press, 1967.

Vine, W. E. *An Expository Dictionary of New Testament Words*. Old Tappan, N.J.: Fleming H. Revell Co., 1966.

Vine, W. E., Merrill F. Unger, and William White Jr. *Vine's Complete Expository Dictionary of Old and New Testament Words*. Nashville: Thomas Nelson, 1985.

Walvoord, John E., ed. *Christian Counseling for Contemporary Problems*. Dallas: Dallas Theological Seminary, 1968.

Walvoord, John F. and Roy B. Zuck. *The Bible Knowledge Commentary: New Testament Edition.* Wheaton: Victor Books, 1983.

Walvoord, John F. *The Holy Spirit.* Grand Rapids: Zondervan, 1958.

Wasson, John, B. Timothy Walsh, Richard Tompkins, Harold Sox Jr., and Robert Pantell. *The Common Symptom Guide,* 2nd ed. New York: McGraw-Hill Book Company, 1984.

Weiner, Howard L. and Lawrence P. Levitt. *Neurology for the House Officer,* 4th ed. Baltimore: Williams & Wilkins, 1989.

Weiner, Howard L. and Lawerence P. Levitt, *Neurology,* 5th ed. Baltimore: Williams & Wilkins, 1994.

Weiner, William J. and Christopher G. Goetz. *Neurology for the Non-Neurologist,* 3rd ed. Philadelphia: J. B. Lippincott Company, 1994.

Weston, Paul. *My Problem with Christianity Is . . .* Wheaton: Harold Shaw Publishers, 1991.

Wheat, Ed and Gaye Wheat. *Intended for Pleasure.* Grand Rapids: Fleming H. Revell, 1981.

Wheat, Ed and Gloria Okes Perkins. *Love Life for Every Married Couple.* Grand Rapids: Zondervan, 1980.

Woodbridge, John D. *Great Leaders of the Christian Church.* Chicago: Moody Press, 1988.

Wortman, Camille and Elizabeth F. Loftus. *Psychology.* New York: McGraw-Hill, 1992.

Yancey, Philip. *Disappointment with God.* New York: Harper Paperbacks, 1988.

Yancey, Philip. *Where Is God When It Hurts.* New York: Harper Paperbacks, 1977.

Youngblood, Ronald F., ed. *Nelson's New Illustrated Bible Dictionary.* Nashville: Thomas Nelson, 1995.

Yudofsky, Stuart C. and Robert E. Hales. *The American Psychiatric Press Textbook of Neuropsychiatry,* 3rd ed. Washington, D.C.: American Psychiatric Association, 1997.

ABOUT THE AUTHOR

Frank B. Minirth, M.D.

Dr. Minirth is a diplomate of the American Board of Psychiatry and Neurology and a diplomate of the American Board of Forensic Medicine. He has been in private practice in the Dallas area since 1975. He holds degrees from Arkansas State University, Arkansas School of Medicine, Dallas Theological Seminary, and Christian Bible College. He holds doctorate degrees in medicine and theology.

Dr. Minirth is president of the Minirth Clinic, P.A., in Richardson, Texas. He is a consultant for the Minirth Christian Group at Green Oaks Behavioral Healthcare Services in Dallas, Texas, and the Minirth Christian Services at Millwood Hospital in Arlington, Texas. He is heard weekly both locally and nationally on radio.

Dr. Minirth has authored or coauthored over fifty books, many of which have been translated into foreign languages. Best-sellers include *Happiness Is a Choice, Love Is a Choice,* and *Love Hunger.* He has over four million books in print.

He and his wife, Mary Alice, have five daughters.

For more information on the Minirth Clinic, call 1–888–646–4784, or visit the Web site at www.minirthclinic.com.